THE
LONG
GAME

THE

HOW THE CHINESE

LONG

NEGOTIATE

GAME

WITH INDIA

VIJAY GOKHALE

VINTAGE

An imprint of Penguin Random House

VINTAGE

USA | Canada | UK | Ireland | Australia
New Zealand | India | South Africa | China

Vintage is part of the Penguin Random House group of companies
whose addresses can be found at global.penguinrandomhouse.com

Published by Penguin Random House India Pvt. Ltd
4th Floor, Capital Tower 1, MG Road,
Gurugram 122 002, Haryana, India

First published in Vintage by Penguin Random House India 2021

Copyright © Vijay Gokhale 2021

10 9 8 7 6 5

This book is a work of non-fiction. The views and opinions expressed in the
book are those of the author only and do not reflect or represent the views
and opinions held by any other person.

This book is based on a variety of sources, including published materials and
research conducted by the author. It reflects the author's own understanding
and conception of such materials and/or can be verified by research.

The objective of this book is not to hurt any sentiments or be biased in favour of or
against any particular person, region, caste, society, gender, creed, nation or religion.

ISBN 9780670095605

Typeset in Baskerville by Manipal Technologies Limited, Manipal
Printed at Replika Press Pvt. Ltd, India

www.penguin.co.in

To the officers of the Indian Foreign Service

Contents

Preface

A Beginning

China is our largest neighbour and the country with which we have had prolonged negotiations on a variety of issues since 1950. This book explores how China negotiated with India from the early years after Independence until the present, and what lessons India may draw from this about negotiating with the Chinese. It explores this through six important events in our bilateral relationship, which covers the period from 1949 to 2019. These are: (1) Recognition by the Government of India of the People's Republic of China on 30 December 1949; (2) the Agreement on Trade and Intercourse between the Tibet Region of China and India of 29 April 1954; (3) India's nuclear tests in 1998; (4) China's formal recognition of Sikkim as a part of India on 11 April 2005; (5) the India–China diplomatic negotiations on the 123 Nuclear Deal in 2008; and (6) the listing of Masood Azhar as a terrorist in the UNSC 1267 Sanctions List on 1 May 2019.

From the Indian perspective such narration might be useful in discerning how China negotiates and also how this might have changed as China accumulates greater power in the international system, as well as the instruments and means that China deploys in the pursuit of its goals.

We've often heard claims being made about the long historical connection between India and China. However, relatively little is known about their diplomatic interaction in the pre-modern age, aside from travelogues of monk-scholars from China to India in the first millennium of the Common Era, and sporadic diplomatic expeditions from Indian kingdoms to the Tang and Song imperial courts from the seventh to the twelfth centuries. More recently, the Chinese government has been highlighting the naval expeditions of Zheng He, in the early fifteenth century, to the Indian Ocean, including the Kerala coast, in order to legitimize their growing presence west of the Malacca Strait. Evidence of an Indian (possibly Tamil) settlement in Quanzhou, in the Fujian province of modern China, also attests to trade links in the mid-second millennium of the Common Era. There is little recorded history of how the two major Indo–Pacific civilizations interacted in political and diplomatic terms. This might be explained by the absence of direct contact across a shared boundary because, despite Chinese claims to suzerainty over Tibet since the thirteenth century (Yuan dynasty), Tibet was mostly left to its own devices. Since China's business with India was mostly through maritime routes, the opportunity and necessity of political interaction was limited.

As the world became more interconnected in the twentieth century, the political distance between India and China began to shrink. The participation of Sikhs and other Indian troops in crushing the Boxer Rebellion in Peking in 1900,[1] as well as their ubiquitous presence among the security forces in the foreign settlements in Shanghai and Hong Kong, shaped Chinese perceptions about Indians. Visits by Indian leaders like Rabindranath Tagore and Jawaharlal Nehru to China in the 1920s and 1930s, and the support lent by the Indian National Congress and the Kuomintang (KMT) to each other during their struggles against the British and the Japanese, also shaped that discourse. The British Empire's push into Tibet for trade and influence, such as the Younghusband Expedition in 1904, led to more frequent diplomatic exchanges and contacts. This was followed by tripartite discussions between the British, Chinese and Tibetans to delineate a boundary line between Inner and Outer Tibet, as well as between Outer Tibet and British India. During the Second World War, India also served as a staging base to send assistance and war material to the Chinese Nationalists led by Generalissimo Chiang Kai-shek, who were fighting the Japanese. Yet, on India's part, these exchanges or activities were controlled by the British Government of India and conducted in the defence of their Empire; Indians, for the most part, were mere bystanders.

Therefore, in the true sense, India's diplomatic activity with China in the modern age really started after 1947, and especially with the founding of the People's Republic of China in 1949. Despite the vast political experience of India's first-generation leadership after Independence, they had had limited opportunities of handling diplomatic relations, and the civil service was trained in the British methods and mindsets of diplomacy. The Chinese Communists, on the other hand, had greater experience in dealing with foreign powers from the 1930s up to 1949, including with Stalin's Soviet Union, which was their fraternal partner, the Americans and the British, who were their allies in the Second World War, as well as the Japanese. Moreover, China had a generally unbroken tradition of diplomacy because, unlike India, it was never directly governed by colonial powers and the Chinese Empire continued to have external relations. The leaderships of India and China were, thus, unevenly matched in terms of diplomatic experience when both became masters of their respective countries at the end of the 1940s.

In 1948, the Republic of China (the precursor to the current Communist government), then still based on the mainland, sent

Dr Luo Jia-Lun as their ambassador to interact with the leaders
of newly independent India. Within a short time, it became
apparent to India that the Communists under Mao Zedong were
overwhelming the Nationalist government led by Chiang Kai-
shek. The Government of India was faced with the question of
whether and when to recognize the new regime in Beijing. Within
three months of Mao declaring from Tiananmen Square the
establishment of the new People's Republic of China (PRC), India
became one of the first countries to switch sides. The first chapter
outlines the facts, how thinking evolved within the Government
of India over the question of according diplomatic recognition to
the new Chinese government, as well as how China approached
this issue. Since this was the first diplomatic act between the two
governments, it has seminal importance in terms of lessons for our
diplomacy.

The Agreement on Trade and Intercourse between the
Tibet Region of China and India of 29 April 1954 was another
seminal event in our relations. Since the early part of the twentieth
century, the British government in India showed interest in trade
and political relations with Tibet. In 1914, after the Chinese
Empire had collapsed, the British government concluded the
Simla Convention and set up arrangements for trade and other
matters directly between the Government of India and the Tibetan
government, on the principle that the 1914 Convention deemed
Tibet to be autonomous in its dealings with the British government
although under the nominal suzerainty of China. In 1950, the
People's Liberation Army (PLA) invaded Tibet in the name of
liberating it. The Government of India was compelled to revisit its
Tibet policy and to open discussions with the People's Republic of
China in regard to the rights and privileges that it had enjoyed as
the successor state to the British Indian government. The Chinese,
on the other hand, looked with suspicion at the policy and actions
of India, and were determined to gain total control over Tibet and

to secure India's recognition of the new reality through a formal agreement. The second chapter looks at the objectives of India and China in Tibet, and their respective diplomatic strategies in meeting those objectives over a region in which both had vital national interests.

The third chapter deals with the diplomatic fall-out of India's five nuclear tests on 11 and 13 May 1998. China's initially anodyne statement after the first two tests on 11 May was followed days later by a full-throated Chinese condemnation, and led to their crafting of an initiative to isolate India internationally. This was not the first occasion for the two sides to interact on nuclear issues— the Chinese tests in the 1960s and the Indian 'peaceful nuclear explosion' in 1974 were part of our earlier diplomatic discourse, but this time it was different. As India and China jousted on the multilateral stage, the chapter examines the strategies that China followed, and how they dealt with India both multilaterally and bilaterally until normal state-to-state relations could be restored in 2001.

The reference by China to Sikkim as a 'State of India' in the India–China Joint Statement of 11 April 2005 concluded a very long and interesting diplomatic negotiation between India and China. This forms the content of the fourth chapter of the book. Differences had cropped up in the 1950s when China introduced deliberate ambiguity into the status of Sikkim, while avoiding any direct discussion of it with India. The fourth chapter looks at how China dealt with India after the merger of Sikkim with India in 1975 changed the status quo, including how both sides drew upon their past experiences to fashion the best possible outcome in the negotiations. It also looks at how China adjusted tactics and negotiating briefs in the pursuit of its objectives.

By 2008 the gap between India and China in terms of comprehensive national power had visibly widened and China was gaining rapidly in stature and influence in the international diplomatic arena. It is in such circumstances that India had to deal with China's objections, in the Nuclear Suppliers Group, to its 123 Nuclear Deal with America. China donned the cape of a crusader for the preservation of the global order, and strongly defended multilateral arrangements and instruments that sanctified its status as a superior power. This fifth chapter deals with how China crafted its diplomatic strategy to try and convince the international community not to make an exception for India on the 123 Deal, and how India's nuanced conduct of diplomacy yielded a desirable outcome.

The last case study, in the sixth chapter, looks at the decade-long effort by India to list Maulana Masood Azhar Alvi, founder of the Pakistan-based Jaish-e-Mohammed terrorist organization, as a terrorist in the UNSC 1267 Sanctions Committee List. India's efforts commenced in 2009 and concluded successfully only on 1 May 2019. The chapter looks at the Chinese strategy and tactics in dealing with India's request to the UN Sanctions Committee as well as the Indian diplomatic efforts across the multilateral and bilateral spectrums.

The final chapter is a summation of the lessons drawn from the six case studies on how China negotiates with India. The objective is to analyse Chinese diplomatic behaviour, to identify the specific threads of Chinese negotiating strategy and to unfold the tools that China employs in its diplomatic negotiations with India.

Open-source material on some of these case studies is difficult to find in China. Nonetheless, there is adequate documentary material available on the Indian side, as well as some foreign sources, which might be used to draw inferences about China's negotiating behaviour. I have been fortunate to be witness to some of these events (except for the two in the 1950s) and hence my personal recollection is also helpful in putting together the narrative. The book is not a purely academic work. It is intended to be a researched account of events, accompanied by analysis that might hold lessons for India in future negotiations with China.

I

Recognition

The decision of the Government of India to recognize the People's Republic of China on 30 December 1949, and to establish diplomatic relations with the new regime on 1 April 1950, was the first diplomatic negotiation between the two sides. Neither side had much accumulated experience with such matters in such an exercise, even though the government of independent India had been in existence since 1947 and the Chinese Communists had had their share of handling foreign powers, including the Soviet Union as well as China's allies—the Americans and the British—during the Second World War.

India had gained her freedom from the British Empire two years earlier on 15 August 1947 and, by the end of 1949, was in the final stages of adopting a Constitution that would establish the new Republic. The country and its leadership enjoyed respect, legitimacy and international stature. The new Communist regime in China, by comparison, had 'liberated' China by using military force to overthrow a legitimate government (the Nationalist government). It needed recognition from the rest of the world to establish its own legitimacy.

In the pre-independence era, the principal political movements in both countries—the Indian National Congress (INC) and the Kuomintang (Nationalists)—had had contact with each other. In 1927, in Brussels, Jawaharlal Nehru and KMT delegates had issued a joint manifesto on mutual cooperation in the anti-imperialist struggle. The INC had maintained these links through the 1930s and used to organize China Days against Japanese Aggression in a show of solidarity with the people of China. The Chinese Communists had also established contact with the INC in the 1930s. It was upon a request from General Zhu De to Nehru in November 1937 that an Indian Medical Mission, which included the legendary Dr Dwarkanath Kotnis, had set out from Bombay (Mumbai) in September 1938 for the Communist war-time base in Yan'an. Nehru desired to have personal contact with Mao Zedong and Zhou Enlai, and this was one reason for his visit to China in August 1939. But since Britain (and France) declared war on Nazi Germany on 3 September 1939, Nehru was forced to cut short his plans and could not meet Mao. He did, nonetheless, keep a brief correspondence with Mao, and was able to meet with some of his associates, including the future PLA Marshal Ye Jianying, in Chungking (Chongqing), the war-time capital of China.[1]

Nehru had a deep interest in international affairs. This was evident in his first important work—*Glimpses of World History*. In this, he would refer to China as a great country and a friend of India. He envisaged a post-colonial world in which the two countries would play a major role in global affairs. By reaching out to the KMT, he was already planning on finding common ground between India and China on important questions. He had conversations about this with President Chiang Kai-shek and his charismatic spouse, Soong Mei-Ling (known as Madame Chiang), when he visited Chongqing in August 1939. Nehru wrote about this visit: 'I returned to India an even greater admirer of China and the Chinese people than I had been previously.'[2] When Chiang

Kai-shek visited India in early February 1942 and met Nehru, he urged the latter to moderate the INC's antipathy to British rule in India. He desperately needed British help, especially critical war supplies, from over the 'Hump'—which was the name for the air route from British India to China over the Himalayas—and felt that the INC's harsh stand against British rule might upset these plans. As a gesture to Nehru, Chiang Kai-shek voiced his support for the cause of self-determination for India after the war. Nehru grew even more firm in his conviction that the two countries would play a significant part in the post-war world order.[3]

Like Nehru, Mao too was greatly interested in international affairs. Even as the Soviet Red Army was preparing to attack Berlin, Mao Zedong was defining the Chinese Communist Party's foreign policy for the post-war world in a document titled 'On Coalition Government' in April 1945. Declaring that the moment was near when the Japanese would be decisively defeated, Mao said that it was China that had led the anti-Japanese war in the Asian mainland, and 'they will also play a very great role in safeguarding peace in the post-war world and the decisive one in safeguarding peace in the East'. In a longish chapter on foreign policy, Mao exhorted the international community to respect China and cautioned the Americans that they were 'committing a gross mistake' by supporting President Chiang Kai-shek. Mao was sympathetic to the freedom struggle of other Asian countries. He referred specifically to India, saying, 'We hope that India will attain independence. For an independent and democratic India is not only needed by the Indian people but is essential for world peace.' However, unlike Nehru, Mao Zedong made no mention of India as a major partner to China, and believed China would be the main guarantor of peace in post-war Asia.[4]

After the independence of India in August 1947, the two countries established embassies. However, the rapid advances by Mao's Communist armies inside China in 1948 meant that there was little bilateral interaction between independent India's new government and the Chinese Nationalist government of Chiang Kai-shek. Nehru keenly followed the developments of China's civil war. By September 1948, Indian Ambassador K.M. Panikkar was reporting to New Delhi about the imminent collapse of President Chiang Kai-shek's regime. The Communist General, Lin Biao, had seized the entire north-eastern region of China and Beijing was poised to fall. To the south, General Liu Bocheng had defeated the Nationalist forces in the Battle of Hsuchow (Suzhou) and was threatening the capital in Nanking (Nanjing). Panikkar informed the Government of India on 2 December 1948 that Chiang's government would, hereon, be 'no more than a phantom or fugitive government'.[5]

Nehru's instincts told him that if a Communist victory was inevitable, India's interests would be better served by establishing early contact with them. Panikkar, with the Indian government's acquiescence, began reaching out to the Chinese Communists. On 5 October 1948, Qiao Guanhua, who headed the Hong Kong branch of the New China News Agency (and was to become China's Foreign Minister in the 1970s), sought instructions from the Communist Party Central Committee on an overture by the Counsellor of the Indian Embassy in Nanking to visit the 'liberated areas'.[6] Signalling his desire to maintain ties with the new regime, Nehru also decided that the Indian Ambassador should not withdraw from China even if the Nationalist government were to collapse.[7] A suggestion from the Nationalist Chinese Ambassador in Turkey to the Indian Ambassador there, for India to mediate between Chiang Kai-shek and Mao Zedong, was rejected by the Government of India. Nehru correctly surmised that the KMT regime was collapsing and that it was a 'bankrupt government in China now'.[8] Facts were to prove the veracity of India's strategic assessment of the internal situation in China. This assessment gave it a head start in building ties with the new regime in China.

Both the Government of India and the Chinese Communist Party began to give serious consideration to such a possibility by the beginning of 1949. They approached this matter, however, from very different perspectives. What were the factors that guided the thinking of the Indian government on this question? Nehru's personal convictions certainly played a part in it. He believed that an Asian resurgence in the post-war period would be possible only with China as a major player. He said so at the Asian Relations Conference in April 1947, on the eve of Indian independence, when he called China 'that great country to which Asia owes so much and from which so much is expected'.[9]

There were other reasons, too, for India to contemplate early recognition of the new Communist regime in China. The first of these was India's northern frontier and its relationship to the status of Tibet. President Chiang Kai-shek's government had, after India's independence, reiterated that Tibet was a part of China, that the Simla Agreement of 1914 was no longer valid, and that it did not acknowledge the McMahon Line as the boundary. The Government of India was aware of the Chinese Communists' intention to 'liberate' Tibet. A report from the Indian Political Officer in Gangtok (Sikkim) to the Ministry of External Affairs, stating that the 'occupation or domination of Tibet by a potentially hostile and possibly aggressive Communist power would be a threat to the security of India', may have added to India's anxieties on this score.[10] The Indian government might have surmised that an early recognition of the new Communist regime would be helpful in securing its goodwill. This would, in turn, be helpful in settling the issue on the frontier. This was understandable logic. Securing the boundary was a legitimate consideration in dealings with the new Chinese regime.

A second consideration, mainly domestic, also appears to have shaped Indian thinking—the growing Communist movement in India. In at least two separate communications in June–July 1949,

in letters to Ambassador Panikkar in Beijing and Ambassador
Vijayalakshmi Pandit in Washington, Nehru voiced his concerns
over Communists in India. Nehru was concerned that any show
of political hostility towards the Chinese Communists might
make it difficult not just to deal with them, but also to handle the
Communists in India. In themselves, these were all reasonable
considerations in the making of policy in favour of the recognition
of the new Chinese regime.

The other major question related to the timing of such
recognition. On 27 September 1949, four days before Mao Zedong
proclaimed the establishment of the new Republic, General (future
Premier) Zhou Enlai met with Ambassador Panikkar in Beijing.
Zhou, according to Panikkar, laid special emphasis on friendship
with India. He also conveyed that there was no difference of view
in regard to Tibet between the two countries, and that he was
particularly anxious to safeguard in every way India's interests
in Tibet. The Indian government took this to mean that the new
Chinese regime was equally eager to build friendly ties with India.
Nehru's instructions to Panikkar were that 'in the first instance,
conversations should take place between China and us regarding
our interests in Tibet and common boundary between Tibet and
India'. He asked Panikkar to give some indication to the Chinese
side (before he officially returned to India since he was no longer
recognized as Indian envoy by the new regime) of India's willingness
to settle matters of common interest through diplomatic negotiation.[11]
This suggested that up until September 1949, Nehru was looking at
achieving outcomes through the process of diplomatic negotiations.

Things began to change from 1 October 1949, after Mao
Zedong proclaimed the formal establishment of the People's
Republic of China. Immediately upon his return to India, Panikkar
began pressing upon the Government of India for early recognition
of the new Chinese regime. Nehru recorded a note to the Ministry
of External Affairs on 17 November 1949 in which he said that 'both

Panikkar and Stevenson are anxious that recognition should be given as early as possible. They think that delay may be injurious'.[12]

However, there were other influential voices in the Government of India that advocated patience in this respect. Chief among them was India's Deputy Prime Minister Vallabhbhai Patel, who felt there was nothing to be gained by early recognition. Panikkar, in his memoirs, mentioned that the Governor General of India, C. Rajagopalachari, had joined Patel in urging Nehru to go slow in the matter.[13] Why were such voices of advice ignored?

For one, the formal establishment of the new regime in China may have hastened consideration of diplomatic recognition. Nehru, and the Government of India, may possibly have seen this as a historic opportunity to stand, as it were, on the right side of history with regard to the Chinese Revolution, which Nehru considered 'a world event of the first magnitude'.[14] Early recognition might also have been seen as being helpful in achieving Nehru's vision of India and China working in friendship for Asian resurgence. For another, Nehru also possibly thought that early recognition might enhance India's global stature and would be one way for India to demonstrate that it was not a junior partner to the Americans or the British. Nehru wrote to Patel conveying that 'it might be desirable for India to accord recognition earlier than some of the others . . . our advisors are of the opinion that it would be definitely harmful to recognize them after the Commonwealth countries have done so. It would mean that we have no policy of our own, but follow the dictates of others.'[15]

A foreign policy decision of this magnitude—recognizing the new government in China as well as the timing of such recognition—ought to have been the outcome of a more deliberative process within the government. The more so because substantive issues, including the northern boundary, were involved. However, the process of institutional consultation within the Government of India on matters of foreign policy was weak. Nehru's letter to Patel in early December 1949 showed this. Nehru wrote: 'If you like I shall put it before the Cabinet. But the date depends on so many factors that it will have to be left open. Most members of the Cabinet have hardly followed these intricate conversations and consultations. But as you are interested, I shall of course consult you before taking action.'[16] The discussion on when and how to recognize the new regime in China appears to have been confined to the tight circle of advisors around the Prime Minister and lacked wider political consultation.

How did the Chinese approach the question of diplomatic relations in general, and especially with India? The Chinese Communist leadership displayed little haste or anxiety on the matter of securing international recognition. In March 1949, when it became clear that their final victory would take place in a matter of months, Mao Zedong declared at the second plenary session of the 7th Central Committee meeting that there should be no rush to secure independent recognition immediately, or even for a considerable period after the final victory.[17] After the Communists overran Nanking (Nanjing), the capital city of the Nationalist government, on 23 April 1949, they first de-recognized all the foreign envoys based in China, and declared them to be ordinary foreigners with no special privileges.[18] Subsequently, they laid down precise conditions for countries wishing to establish diplomatic relations with the new regime, through the interim Constitution, known as the 'Common Programme', which the New Chinese People's Political Consultative Committee had adopted in mid-1949. The Common Programme stipulated that the Chinese central government would negotiate with any foreign government that was willing to sever all relations with the KMT and was ready to adopt a friendly attitude towards the PRC, provided that such relations would be established on the basis of equality, mutual benefit and mutual respect for territorial sovereignty. These conditions were reiterated in a subsequent official communication that was sent to foreign governments after the People's Republic of China was established on 1 October 1949.[19]

Thus the Communists made it mandatory for any country wishing to have diplomatic relations with the new government in Beijing, to withdraw all recognition from the Chiang Kai-shek regime; it was to be either full recognition of the People's Republic of China or nothing. In this way, the new rulers of China laid down their 'red lines' on the issue of diplomatic relations. Mao Zedong summed up his approach by telling Soviet dictator Josef Stalin on 16 December 1949: '. . . we believe that we should not rush to be recognized. We must first bring order to the country, strengthen our position and then we can talk to foreign imperialists.'[20] It was a methodical approach. China gained a small advantage by not putting itself under any pressure of time.

The Chinese also planned the negotiations with India with great care, seeing it as a template for future negotiations with other non-socialist countries, including the West. Their strategy consisted of three elements: (1) to make India recognize the People's Republic of China as the sole, legitimate government. Mao was determined not to allow Two Chinas to legally exist at the same time, and this was a core objective; (2) to ensure that India did not join the American-led anti-China camp. Since the Americans were backing Chiang Kai-shek, it stood to reason that India should be asked to prove that it was not an American camp-follower by making a clean break with Chiang Kai-shek and the Nationalist regime; and (3) to utilize India's international influence to gain diplomatic space. The Soviet Ambassador N.V. Roshchin recorded his conversation with Mao thus: 'During the past few days he (Mao Zedong) had received the report from Beijing that the governments of Burma and India expressed their readiness to recognize the government of the People's Republic of China. The position of the Chinese government on this matter is as follows: to inform the governments of Burma and India that if they are sincere in their wishes to mend diplomatic relations with the PRC, first, they must completely break all ties with Jiang Jieshi (Chiang Kai-shek), unconditionally refuse any kind of support and assistance to this regime, making it into an official declaration. Under the condition that the governments of these countries accept the aforementioned proposals of the Chinese government, the Indian and Burmese governments may send their representatives to Beijing for negotiations.'[21] This, then, was the Chinese strategy, and the tactics were determined accordingly.

India's strategy was far less clear than that of China, although it had the stronger hand to play. Recognition of a new regime by the world at large is the highest form of international legitimacy. It, thus, gives considerable leverage to the recognizing state to secure its own interests vis-à-vis the new regime. The leverage that the state may have is also proportionate to its own international standing; the greater its global reputation and stature, the more desirable it becomes to the party that is seeking to secure its support. In this regard, India was in a position of great advantage. Not only was it looked upon by the West as a shining example of democracy in the Third World and as a leading country in Asia in the aftermath of the Second World War, Prime Minister Nehru also had international stature and commanded the respect of his peers. India, thus, held adequate international political capital to secure its interests vis-à-vis the new regime in China. The matter would now hinge on India's strategies and tactics in the diplomatic negotiations.

Nehru's instructions to Panikkar in September 1949, before he returned to India, was that the latter should raise with the Chinese side the issue of the frontier between India and Tibet, as well as matters concerning India's special privileges in Tibet (which it had inherited from Great Britain in 1947). Nehru's message indicated that the Government of India was thinking of making the boundary question and the status of Tibet a part of the negotiations with China on diplomatic recognition. This made good sense. If the Chinese Communists intended to make good on their declaration to reclaim Tibet, it would have security implications for India's northern frontier. Secretary General of the Ministry of External

Affairs Girija Shankar Bajpai put it thus: 'We cannot, however, without the most careful consideration give up the special relationship that we have had with Tibet. My provisional view is that this is one of the matters to be taken into account when we take up with the Communist regime, the question of recognition.'[22] The government was also aware of China's pre-conditions for the establishment of diplomatic relations. It was logical for India, too, to lay down its requirements as part of the negotiation.[23]

However, eventually, this did not happen. Within the Government of India, there were two views about discussing the status of Tibet with the Chinese. There were those who felt that such a discussion could re-open the whole question about whether Tibet was independent or a part of China, and call into doubt the agreement between British India and Tibet on the McMahon Line. Panikkar weighed in on this debate by saying that since the Chinese had not raised this matter with the Indian side, it was prudent to proceed on the assumption that the new regime did not intend to rake up the historical past of India's northern frontier. Nehru was persuaded by this line of reasoning. And so, by November 1949, instead of focusing on identifying tangible demands for the Chinese side to meet, the Government of India turned the whole debate on recognition of the new Chinese regime into a question of timing. In his note to Bajpai on 17 November 1949, Nehru declared, 'It is clear that recognition has to be given. The only question that arises is that of timing. In regard to timing also there are limitations at either end.'[24]

What happened to make the timing of the recognition dependent not upon securing national priorities but on the calendar? There was more than one reason for this. Foremost among them was that the formal establishment of the People's Republic of China on 1 October 1949 made the question of recognition time-sensitive. Nehru had always felt that India should recognize Communist China as early as possible as this would give it some leverage in building strong relations with the country. He grew anxious over the possibility of the British government or the governments of other Commonwealth countries recognizing China before India did. He would then be seen as a camp-follower of the British instead of a world statesman. The Chinese state-run media had already irked the Government of India by alleging that India was a 'lackey' of the capitalist bloc. His concerns were magnified by the American attempts to create a like-minded community of Asian countries, which Nehru felt would be 'honestly regarded or wilfully misrepresented as designed to promote formation of anti-Communist bloc in Asia.'[25] So concerned was Nehru with avoiding a misunderstanding with China on this matter that he wrote to President Sukarno of Indonesia in December 1949 to tell him that India was not proposing to join up with any international activity that might appear to be against China. He urged Indonesia to follow suit.[26] Finally, public and diplomatic pressure had begun to mount on the Government of India for rendering some form of assistance to the Tibetan government, and Nehru wanted to avoid giving any impression to China that India would act in bad faith on the Tibet issue.

For all these reasons, the timing of the recognition became the focal point for the Government of India. Other, more tangible objectives relating to India's interests or concerns, including the northern frontier and the status of Tibet, which might have formed an important part of the negotiating strategy during the talks with China, were nowhere to be seen. This might also explain why there was no reference in Prime Minister Nehru's note of 17 November 1949 on what specific outcomes India wanted from the negotiations with China for diplomatic recognition, beyond the fact of the recognition itself.

The Government of India also made another presumption, which was erroneous and would prove disadvantageous to India in the negotiations. India assumed that its official declaration recognizing the People's Republic of China would automatically mean that both sides had also established formal diplomatic relations. This led the Government of India to believe that there would still be time and opportunities after the recognition of the new regime, to raise matters of concern or pursue national security objectives through diplomatic channels. In other words, whereas the Chinese saw the process of recognition as a matter of substantive negotiation, India considered it simply a matter of protocol. The idea was to win Chinese goodwill as soon as possible. The assumption that China also saw recognition as a routine matter was not based on facts or solid evidence. It might have been prudent to at least gauge the Chinese thinking in this regard. India had the means to do so because the Government had shown foresight in retaining some of the Indian diplomats in China even after the collapse of the Nationalist government, precisely in order to establish contact with the new regime. Despite this, the services of A.K. Sen, India's chief liaison officer in Nanking, were not enlisted in ascertaining Chinese thinking and expectations. Had Sen done that, India might have realized that China regarded the act of official recognition as a distinct process from the subsequent act of formal establishment of diplomatic relations. India might then have adopted a very different strategy.

The lapses on India's part—the absence of wider political consultations within the Indian leadership, the overlooking of its national interest in its anxiety over the timing, and the erroneous assumption that the act of officially recognizing the People's Republic of China was tantamount to the automatic establishment of formal diplomatic relations—led the Government of India to see the act of recognition as its only objective. In the process, India unilaterally gave up some crucial negotiating cards. First, India severed ties with the Nationalist government in Taiwan. The Prime Minister directed the Foreign Secretary to 'send for Doctor Lo (the Ambassador of Nationalist China in New Delhi). Tell him of our decision. Tell him also that it is with deep regret that we have to sever our official relations with him.'[27]

The cutting off of ties with the Nationalist government in Taiwan was inevitable, but it should have been part of the give-and-take during the negotiations. Instead, India squandered a bargaining point as a concession to Communist China even before the negotiations commenced. Likewise, India made efforts to reassure the Chinese side that it would not harm them by aligning with the Americans. This meant that India gave up any leverage that was to be gained by allowing the Chinese side to believe that it had the option of leaning to the side of the Americans in case China did not accommodate its interests in the process of diplomatic recognition. Thus, India lost another tactical advantage that might have allowed it to extract assurances from the Chinese Communists.

Thirdly, and most significantly, India did not lay out substantive 'asks' for the Chinese side to fulfil as a counter-response to their demands, even though they were aware of Chinese preconditions. The Government of India felt that making recognition dependent upon fulfilment of conditions by the new Chinese regime may be seen as hard or humiliating. Instead, Zhou Enlai's oral assurance to Panikkar over a dinner at the end of September 1949 that Indian interests in Tibet would be protected was considered an adequate enough guarantee to secure India's interests. The lament by the Indian Political Officer in Gangtok to the Secretary in the Ministry of External Affairs on 20 October 1949—'when the time comes to recognize the Communist government it should be stated in general terms that such recognition is without prejudice to existing rights and commitments of the Government of India; but the present view of the Government of India appears to be that recognition should be unconditional'—went unheeded.[28]

India's approach to the whole idea of recognition was a mixture of emotionalism and conjecture. There was no strategy. The timing became the central point of the exercise. This too was determined by the international calendar rather than by India's national interests. The Commonwealth Foreign Ministers Conference was to be held in Colombo in mid-January 1950. Nehru decided that India should recognize the People's Republic of China before the other members of the Commonwealth. It was accordingly decided to do so on 30 December 1949.

When Zhou Enlai received Nehru's telegram of India's decision to recognize the People's Republic of China, he consulted Mao Zedong, who was on a secret visit to Moscow, and informed Nehru on 4 January 1950 of China's willingness to establish relations on the basis of equality, mutual benefit and mutual respect for territorial sovereignty. They added one caveat. Zhou proposed that the Government of China expected the representative of India to travel to Beijing to negotiate on the matter of formal establishment of diplomatic relations.[29] It became apparent to the Government of India that their original presumption, that recognition of the new regime in China in and of itself would automatically mean the establishment of diplomatic relations, was not correct. The Chinese wanted to negotiate formally. They also wanted the negotiation to be in China, which was unusual since the Chinese were the supplicants. India ought to have asked China to send their representative to Delhi for this purpose. A.K. Sen, the Indian liaison officer in China, had also informed the government that the Soviet bloc countries were not being asked to follow a similar practice of going to Beijing for negotiations. Thus, Chinese actions vis-à-vis India did not appear to speak the language of friendship and were more reminiscent of an older Chinese imperial tradition of managing relations with tributary states.

Yet, with the Colombo meeting of the Commonwealth Foreign Ministers only days away, time was slipping away and the Government of India instructed Sen to proceed to Beijing for the negotiations. India thus lost further ground by conceding the right to determine the venue and agenda to the Chinese side. He was apparently given no specific instructions on India's expectations from China. India continued to see the whole issue as a matter of protocol. Sen was told that his only task was to reach an agreement on the modalities for the exchange of ambassadors and embassies, and nothing more. No substantive matter was to be discussed at all; all such matters, if the Chinese raised any, were to be referred back to Delhi. For good measure, Nehru also telegraphed Zhou Enlai on 17 January 1950, reiterating that the purpose of Sen's journey to Beijing would be limited to discussion on the establishment of diplomatic missions.[30] The Indian negotiator's hands were tied. He would not be able to raise any specific matter of interest to India, nor would he be able to prevent the Chinese from doing so, because India wanted a positive outcome of the talks and could not countenance a deadlock. Thus, another opportunity to review and re-set the strategy and tactics for negotiations, this time over the establishment of formal diplomatic relations, came and went without proper consideration.

The Chinese side handled the issue of recognition and diplomatic relations very differently. Nehru's message to Zhou Enlai led to considerable internal discussion within the Chinese leadership about what India's motives might be. Liu Shaoqi, who was the ranking leader in Beijing in the absence of Mao Zedong (who was away in the Soviet Union), felt that Nehru's response was similar to a message that had been delivered to the Chinese by the British Liaison in Beijing, on the question of Britain recognizing the new regime in China. On 16 January 1950 (one day prior to Nehru's message to Zhou Enlai), Callaghan had told the Chinese Foreign Ministry that Great Britain regarded the exchange of letters between the two governments as constituting the establishment of diplomatic relations, and that there was no further matter to discuss in this regard other than the technicalities relating to the exchange of Ambassadors.[31] Liu Shaoqi told Mao and other Chinese leaders that the similarity in the positions of India and Great Britain suggested the possibility of collusion between them. In his view, the British were using India to test the waters on whether China would seek concessions on substantive issues like Hong Kong from Britain as part of the process of diplomatic recognition.[32]

After deliberating over Liu Shaoqi's concerns about possible Anglo-Indian collusion, Mao, who was away in Moscow, felt that it was even more important to pay close attention to the negotiations with India, because it would become a template for all subsequent negotiations on diplomatic relations with non-socialist countries, including with Great Britain. Mao made three phone calls to Liu Shaoqi on 20 January 1950 on this matter.[33] It was decided that China should not display any anxiety or eagerness to discuss or resolve substantive issues, or else India and Britain might try to leverage diplomatic relations to extract Chinese concessions on issues like Hong Kong or Tibet. Mao decided to take advantage of India's keenness to establish relations in order to secure other objectives. On Mao's personal direction, a reply to Nehru's letter of 17 January 1950 was sent by Vice Foreign Minister Li Kenong on 20 January 1950. It stated that there was no important issue that needed to be negotiated before the exchange of ambassadors. Nehru took this to mean that Tibet would not be discussed. But he failed to recognize that the Chinese had other specific objectives in mind. Unlike the Chinese leadership, there was little introspection, consultation or strategizing within the Indian political leadership. The workings of the two governments in the first twenty days of January 1950 would show that while one of them, China, was engaged in constant consultation and adjustment of tactics, the other, India, neither consulted nor felt the need to test presumptions against the responses they received from China. It reflected internal weakness in the governance of Indian foreign policy and lack of experience in international negotiation.

When Sen arrived in Beijing on 13 February it became immediately apparent that for China, the negotiations were not

simply procedural or of the nature of protocol. Vice Minister
Zhang Hanfu posed two substantive questions to Sen and insisted
that the Government of India would need to clarify both matters
before China even discussed the establishment of relations. The
two Chinese questions were: first, whether India was ready to
completely break off all contact with the KMT, including the
remnants in India, and to transfer complete ownership of all KMT
assets and funds in India to the People's Republic of China?;
and second, whether India unambiguously upheld the People's
Republic of China's membership in the United Nations and all
its bodies, by virtue of them being the sole representative of the
Chinese people? These were fresh demands; they went beyond
the preconditions that China had conveyed to foreign countries
on the question of diplomatic relations. The Chinese side also
mounted pressure by complaining to Sen that India's abstention
on a resolution moved by the Soviet Union in the Economic and
Social Council (ECOSOC) on 7 February 1950 showed that India
still continued to recognize the legitimacy of the representatives
of the old Nationalist regime in the UN. The resolution sought to
remove the Republic of China (ROC) from the ECOSOC and
to give the seat to the People's Republic of China instead. The
Chinese tactic was to goad the Indian side into being explicit in
their rejection of the Chiang Kai-shek regime.

The Chinese surmised, correctly as it turned out, that India's
keenness to declare an official relationship with the new regime
might lead to them agreeing to new demands. Even at this point,
India compounded the lapse by not using the opportunity to either
push back on the new demands or to place counter-demands. It
can only be presumed that, by then, the haste to conclude the
process had clouded India's judgement, as Mao had foreseen. The
Chinese used the time-pressure in which India had voluntarily
placed itself, by conducting the talks in Beijing in such a manner
as to cause anxiety to India. On 1 March 1950, India agreed to the

new demands and Sen confirmed that India did not recognize any remnant of the old regime in India as legitimate representatives of China, and that India was willing to transfer all official Chinese properties and funds in India to the new Chinese government, and that India considered it to be legitimate and proper for China to participate in all UN bodies and activities. Even then, the Chinese side took a full fifteen days before they consented to begin talks with India on the modalities for the establishment of diplomatic relations. Mao, with an eye on the long-term, was not only able to secure India's consent to follow the One-China policy, which was the original precondition, but also to secure entirely new demands. China made this the template for its relations with all other nations. Diplomatic relations were finally established on 1 April 1950. K.M. Panikkar, India's Ambassador to Chiang Kai-shek's China, returned as Ambassador to Mao Zedong's China in May 1950.

In 1952, Zhou Enlai would summarize the experience of negotiating with India by saying that, 'for capitalist countries and their former colonies, one must go through the formalities of negotiations to see whether they accept the principle for establishing diplomatic relations. We must not only listen to what they say, but also see their specific actions. For example, if they do not vote for China in the UN but instead support the reactionary Chiang Kai-shek regime, then we should go slow in establishing diplomatic relations with them.'[34]

The decision by India to sever ties with Nationalist China and to recognize the People's Republic of China might have meant that India was only acknowledging the reality, but it was coupled with a poverty of tactics. If the act of jettisoning Chiang and the Nationalists was unsentimental and calculating, early recognition of the successor regime does not appear to have been motivated by anything more than sentiment and the expectations of goodwill. Had India's position not been driven by emotion and sentiment, the course of the negotiation may have been different with more tangible results. The poverty of tactics was to have irreversible consequences for India. China, on the other hand, started out with a weak hand but crafted a strategy based on clear objectives and proper study of the adversary. There was also a regular review and readjustment of tactics, as when the Chinese paused in early January 1950 to study whether India and Britain were colluding on the matter of diplomatic recognition. Internal decisions were based on facts. They did not proceed on presumption. China never put itself under pressure of time either, unlike India, nor allowed success to be measured in terms of the act of recognition by itself, but rather by securing the opposite side's adherence to the larger principles that it enunciated.

China benefitted significantly from the establishment of diplomatic relations with India. Recognition by India meant that America could not rope India into any anti-Communist front that might encircle China, and friendship with India was viewed by the Chinese as part of their larger strategy of creating an anti-American united front.[35] It also meant that India's prestige and standing in the world could be leveraged by China to make inroads into the international community and to expand China's diplomatic space, especially among the Third World countries, in the early 1950s. India also sponsored and supported the People's Republic of China's claim to be given the Chinese seat in the United Nations and its Security Council. Most importantly for China, India's recognition provided the space for China to prepare for the invasion of Tibet in late 1950, secure in the knowledge that diplomatic relations would make it much harder, if not impossible, for India to interfere in the process.

What did India gain from the early recognition of China? India's international stature received a temporary boost. As a result of the good relations with both China and America, India played a role in the Korean peninsula. Nehru may have gained in personal stature. However, India squandered the first-mover advantage by not seeking substantive gains. India's recognition neither secured the friendship of China nor the security of India's northern frontier. The Chinese state-run media continued to attack India and Nehru throughout 1950 as a lackey of the Anglo-Americans. And, declassified Chinese documents show that the Chinese Communists deeply distrusted Nehru and India even when they had recognized the People's Republic of China. They continued to suspect that India had sinister motives with regard to Tibet. After the invasion, they alleged that India had interfered in China's internal affairs, leading Patel to comment that 'even though we regard ourselves as friends of China, the Chinese do not regard us as their friends'. Neither did the establishment of diplomatic relations guarantee the security of India. As Patel put it, 'The undefined state of the frontier and the existence on our side of a population with its affinities to the Tibetans or Chinese have all the elements of the potential trouble between China and ourselves.'[36]

To some extent, the performance of India in this first important negotiation with China could be put down to a lack of experience in diplomatic negotiations. The Chinese had an advantage. They not only had an unbroken tradition of diplomatic experience because they never fully lost their independence and continued to engage with outside powers, but Mao Zedong and Zhou Enlai had also practiced diplomacy with the Soviets, the Americans and the Japanese through the 1930s and 1940s. India's leadership, on the other hand, had little hands-on knowledge of the conduct of diplomacy, and the problem was compounded because of a faulty strategy that was not anchored in good intelligence about Chinese calculations, and was overdependent on Nehru's personal preferences and intuitions rather than on any consultation. Nonetheless, the way both parties approached the issue contains important lessons.

The Chinese identified clear objectives before the start of the negotiations, publicly spelt them out and built their strategy accordingly. Their leadership maintained close and continuous consultation through the entire process (even when Mao was travelling abroad) and adjusted tactics as required. India neither had concrete objectives nor clear 'asks' from the Chinese side. Strategy was defined not in terms of identified outcomes, but in terms of the international calendar. Tactics were decided accordingly. There is no indication that there was serious political level consultation in the Government of India on this issue. The Prime Minister and the Ministry of External Affairs appeared to decide the policy. India gained little tangible benefit from the entire exercise.

In 1972, when China found itself in the position that India was in 1949, on the question of according recognition to the new nation of Bangladesh, Zhou had this to say to American President Richard Nixon: 'We will probably recognize Bangladesh later on. Perhaps we will be the last one. Our reasons for that have to do with two questions. The first is the withdrawal of troops from both East and West Pakistan. The second thing is, it would not do for them (India) to proclaim that the problem of Kashmir is already settled because the UN hasn't agreed and we still have observers there.'[37] China did not allow the clock to put pressure on them, nor did they shy away from articulating their expectations from not just Bangladesh but also from India.

One question remains to be answered. Why did China not raise the Tibet issue with India? It was very much a core Chinese concern in 1949. Possibly, their first priority may have been to secure their south-western border in anticipation of American hostility, and to sever India's ties with the Americans so that they could not use India to contain China. Since the Chinese did not physically control Tibet in 1949, they might also have felt that they did not have a strong enough hand at that point in time with which to negotiate on the matter with India.

II

Tibet: The Price of Friendship

The first major negotiation following the establishment of diplomatic relations was on the issue of Tibet. It was the core issue in India–China relations almost from the establishment of the People's Republic of China. It culminated in the signing of the Agreement on Trade and Intercourse between the Tibet Region of China and India on 29 April 1954. The Chinese Communists had already declared their intention of expelling the Nationalists from all parts of China after the end of the Second World War, and uniting the country, including its minorities, under New China. More than one source has confirmed that it was Mao Zedong's intention to launch a military campaign on Tibet immediately after the new Republic was formally established. The Chinese Communists were aware of the attempt of the Tibetan authorities to seek independence for Tibet from China with the support of India and the West. They felt that after independence, India was continuing to pursue the British imperialist policy with regard to Tibet.

These developments helped prompt the new Chinese government to mount a military invasion on Tibet immediately after taking over power in China. Mao initially gave this responsibility

to General (later Marshal) Peng Dehuai, who was in charge of
north-west China, but General Peng demurred due to difficult
climatic conditions and terrain (the Xinjiang-Tibet highway
through Aksai Chin had not yet been built). The liberation of
Tibet was eventually entrusted to Deng Xiaoping who headed the
south-western Bureau.[1] Within a month of Mao's proclamation
establishing the People's Republic of China, from the Tiananmen
Rostrum on 1 October 1949, the Soviet Ambassador in Beijing,
N.V. Roshchin, recorded in his diary that Premier Zhou Enlai had
informed him about Chinese plans to attack Tibet immediately
after the liberation of Sichuan and Xinjiang.[2] The Chinese
objective was clear and simple, but the task was complex. For one,
the Chinese were not physically present inside Tibet, which had,
for all practical purposes, been autonomous since the fall of the
Qing Empire in 1911. The Chinese liaison mission had also been
expelled by the Tibetans in July 1949. Secondly, the Communists
also faced formidable logistics issues in getting troops and supplies
into Tibet. Thirdly, the Americans were openly hostile towards
the new Chinese regime.

The Communist leadership felt the Americans may exploit
Tibet's desire for independence. In this context they considered it
possible that India, which they deemed to be a 'capitalist' country,
might facilitate American assistance of Tibetan independence
if they delayed the takeover of Tibet. Mao himself did not have
a positive attitude towards Prime Minister Jawaharlal Nehru
or India. In his letter to the Communist Party of India General
Secretary, B.T. Ranadive, on 19 November 1949, he called Nehru
an 'imperialist collaborator'.[3] Distrust of Indian intentions was
thus a factor in the decision to invade Tibet.

India's recognition of China came at an opportune time for the
Chinese plans for Tibet. Deng Xiaoping, who was in overall charge
of the south-western region, had written to the Central Committee
on 1 January 1950, proposing to dispatch the Eighteenth Army

into Tibet in the summer or fall of 1950. In his reply to Deng on 10 January 1950, Mao expressed his agreement, saying that India's recognition was favourable to the proposed plan.[4] Mao was on a secret visit to Moscow at the time, and used this opportunity to seek Josef Stalin's assistance on logistics for the planned Chinese invasion of Tibet. He wanted the Soviet air regiment to remain in China a while longer so that the authorities in Beijing could transport provisions to General Liu Bocheng's Second Field Army troops that were preparing the attack on Tibet.[5] Having secured Stalin's readiness to consider the matter, the Central Committee of the Communist Party of China formally issued orders for the 18th Army to enter Tibet in either the summer or fall of 1950. Tibet's fate was decided in early 1950.

The issue of Tibet also dominated the thinking within the Government of India, especially from the perspective of the boundary. India was aware of the efforts by the Nationalist government of Chiang Kai-shek to mount an international campaign in the mid-1940s to portray Tibet as a Chinese province, as well as its unwillingness to recognize the Simla Agreement of 1914, which India considered to have finalized its boundary with Tibet along the McMahon Line. In October 1947, the Nationalist government in Nanking informed the Indian Embassy of its wish to modify such agreements as were entered into between Great Britain and Tibet, including the Simla Agreement, 1914, that defined India's frontier with Tibet. In the same month, the Dalai Lama's government in Lhasa had also addressed a letter to India's Prime Minister seeking the return of 'all our indisputable Tibetan territories gradually included into India', which included parts of modern-day Arunachal Pradesh, Ladakh, Darjeeling, Sikkim and Bhutan.[6]

Hence, in early February 1948, the Government of India had considered it necessary to make it clear to the Nationalist Chinese Ambassador in Delhi, that the previous treaties remained in force and that India regarded itself as having replaced Great Britain in regard to all treaty rights and obligations that previously existed between Great Britain and Tibet.[7] Nonetheless, there was unease in India over the refusal of the Chinese government to accept the McMahon Line, and this question became more acute when a Communist victory in China became a distinct possibility. Yet, unlike Mao, Nehru did not have a negative image of China. In fact, he regarded a revitalized China as essential for Asian resurgence, and as a partner of India.

Thus, in early 1950, both China and India had clear objectives in Tibet. China's was to seize Tibet, to extinguish its autonomy and to legitimize the People's Republic of China's absolute control over Tibet. India's objective was to preserve the status quo to the maximum possible extent and to legitimize its boundary with Tibet. The two countries adopted very different strategies in the pursuit of their objectives. A description of facts is required in order to understand the manner in which both pursued their objectives, the strategies that each adopted and their outcomes.

China's strategy was to deal with the Tibet issue in a step-by-step fashion. Its immediate priority was to secure the physical possession of Tibetan territory, for which it had already set the wheels in motion in January 1950. In order to achieve this objective, they pursued two strategies—to deter collusion between America and India, and to prevent Indian assistance to the Tibetan government. Tactics were decided accordingly. They adopted a soft and conciliatory approach while they prepared for the invasion. The Chinese allowed India to believe that it could play a 'mediatory' role in peacefully resolving the Tibet issue. The Government of India was persuaded to encourage the Tibetan government to open negotiations with the new Chinese regime. Even as plans for the invasion were well underway, Premier Zhou Enlai told Panikkar in August 1950 that Beijing was anxious for a peaceful settlement.[8] Zhou also kept Panikkar, and Nehru, engaged on other international affairs with them; Zhou, for instance, would have long discussions with Panikkar on the situation in Formosa (Taiwan), Korea and China's case for membership of the United Nations.

The Chinese tactic was to distract India from thinking about a worst-case scenario on Tibet until it was too late for India to come to Tibet's assistance or to contemplate any coordinated action against China in the international arena. Detaching India from the Americans was their other priority while planning the invasion of Tibet. India's recognition of China was helpful, but suspicion about Indian intentions remained. Hence, from time to time, the state-run Chinese media would goad Nehru and India by questioning whether its foreign policy was really independent. Nehru would be labelled an 'imperialist lackey' who was helping in an Anglo-American plot to annex Tibet. By doing so, the Chinese hoped to play on India's anxiety about its international image as an independent power. It had the effect of compelling Nehru on more than one occasion to provide reassurances that India had neither material nor territorial ambitions in Tibet. This assurance was even provided in writing in the form of an Aide Memoire.

Thus, through a strategy of distraction and deception, China was able to ensure that until the invasion of Tibet began in October 1950, India never directly raised matters of its own interest or concern in Tibet with the Chinese side. Once the invasion began, India publicly expressed 'its deep regret that in spite of the friendly and disinterested advice repeatedly tendered by them, the Chinese government should have decided to seek a solution of the problem of their relations with Tibet by force'.[9] The Chinese neatly turned the tables by alleging that it was all India's fault that negotiations between the Chinese and Tibetans could not take place because of 'outside instigation'.

The Government of India's strategy in pursuance of its objective of legitimizing the frontier and retaining all the rights and privileges that it had inherited in Tibet from the British Empire, was crafted differently. The Government of India's official agents in Tibet regularly sent reports about the inevitability of a Chinese invasion, and recommended that India should meet Tibet's requirement of arms and ammunition, and extend its diplomatic and political support to the Tibetan government. H. Dayal, India's political officer in Sikkim, advised the government in New Delhi that once the Communist armies had occupied Tibet, it would encourage them to press their country's long-standing claims to portions of Assam and revive pretentions to suzerainty over the Himalayan states. Dayal went on to add that it might also be too late then to negotiate with the Chinese on Indian interests there, and that even the continuance of the Indian Mission in Lhasa would come into question.[10] However, in New Delhi, a different set of considerations dictated India's policy.

The Government of India felt that the Communist regime was there to stay and it was desirable to have cordial relations with this new regime. India's Political Officer in Gangtok, H. Dayal, who was familiar with the Himalayan region and its politics, was concerned that the larger objective of good relations with the Communist regime in China should not deter India from at least flagging its position on the Tibetan issue. 'The Government of India, for their part, have already given ample proof of their anxiety to respect Chinese sentiment, but they should not sacrifice their own interests in Tibet, or fail in their obligations to the Tibetan government, through fear that their interest in the Tibetan Question might be distasteful to the new Government of China,' Dayal wrote on 29 June 1950.[11] However, the response that was sent from New Delhi to Gangtok on 18 July 1950, which was to become the core of the Government's policy on Tibet, stated, 'The Government of India are of the opinion that the best hope of an amicable solution of the Tibet problem lies in firmly establishing friendship and understanding between India and China. This will enable us when the time comes, to safeguard our interests in Tibet and to discuss the status of Tibet, free from rancour and from past encumbrances.'[12]

This meant that India began to follow a dual strategy. On the one hand, in order to preserve its position on the boundary question, India publicly reiterated that all treaties between China and Great Britain would continue to remain in force, and voiced its support for Tibet's autonomy. On the other hand, it adopted a cautious attitude towards all Tibetan requests for assistance, whether it was their demand for arms and ammunition or for sponsorship of a resolution in the United Nations, for fear of upsetting the Chinese regime. The strategy did not permit India to raise its own concerns over Tibet with the Chinese through political or diplomatic channels, although there were voices within the Indian government that felt that after the PLA took over Tibet, it might be too late to negotiate these matters with China. This was the second lost opportunity to secure Indian interests in Tibet through negotiation, after India's failure to raise it as part of the process of diplomatic recognition. At that point in time, it appeared that the Government of India may not have wanted to give any opportunity to the new Chinese regime to open an issue that it regarded as closed—the boundary issue. Nor did Indian strategy allow for any serious consideration of giving possible material support to Tibet. Even if India may not have had the financial means to give the sort of military assistance that might have made a difference, it could have maintained ambiguity on this point. Deception is a legitimate tactic in diplomacy and negotiation. Instead, the Government of India instructed its ambassador in Beijing to explicitly underscore to Zhou Enlai that China need not have apprehensions of danger to Chinese security from the side of Tibet which adjoined India.[13] The Government of India felt that openness would help dispel any lingering Chinese doubts over Indian intentions.

India also adopted the tactic of appealing to China's good sense by pointing out to them that any military action on their part would complicate the international situation for the new government of China, including their efforts to enter the United Nations. Since this was of no consequence to the Chinese in pursuance of their objective of subduing Tibet, India's advice fell on deaf ears. The irony was that the Chinese never viewed India's efforts at peaceful resolution or its advice to China to be mindful of their international reputation, as anything other than deceitful. A declassified cable sent by the Chinese Foreign Ministry to its envoys in November 1950 shows that the Chinese government all along was of the opinion that India's real intention was to interfere in China's internal affairs, to prevent the liberation of Tibet, and try to maintain Indian privileges in Tibet.[14] In this first phase of the negotiation on Tibet, Indian strategy was a defensive one. It did not, however, stop the Chinese invasion. In October 1950, just as Deng Xiaoping had planned at the beginning of the year, the PLA attacked Tibet and began the process of extinguishing Tibet's independence and autonomy.

China's military intervention in Tibet was a new situation for India. Deputy Prime Minister Patel's letter to Prime Minister Nehru on 7 November 1950 laid out the challenge in stark terms. Not only did Patel consider China as having deluded India by professions of peaceful intention, but he declared that China was not a friend but a potential enemy. Patel, therefore, recommended that India give its immediate attention to dealing with some of the potential problems, among which he listed the India–Tibet boundary (McMahon Line) as well as the future of the Indian presence inside Tibet that India had inherited from the British Empire. The Chinese envoy in Delhi had already, in his meeting with Foreign Secretary K.P.S. Menon on 2 November 1950, conveyed that China did not recognize the Indian privileges in Tibet. The Chinese ambassador declared that these were unauthorized and violated the principle of sovereignty and territorial integrity. This was quite different from the verbal assurance that Zhou had reportedly given Panikkar in September 1949.[15] The post-invasion scenario offered good reason for the Government of India to undertake a comprehensive review of strategy and tactics. Since the Chinese ambassador in New Delhi had indicated that the new regime would not respect earlier agreements, it gave rise to opportunity to raise matters concerning Tibet as well.

The period between November 1950 and the end of 1951 marked the second phase of the India–China negotiations over Tibet. China continued with its step-by-step approach. They realized that merely obtaining physical possession of Tibet by force did not guarantee China's position in Tibet. Their next objective was to legitimize China's control over Tibet and physically consolidate their presence on the ground since the PLA was thinly spread in some parts of Tibet. The aim was to quell domestic (Tibetan) opposition and to neutralize the possibility of any external support for the Tibetan resistance forces. The Chinese, therefore, opened 'negotiations' with the Tibetan government. In May 1951, they signed the 17-Point Agreement that nominally gave Tibet an autonomous status, although the opening sentence was explicit in stating that Tibet lay within the boundaries of China.

The Tibetan government was reduced to being a local government. The Chinese saw the 17-Point Agreement as only a partial achievement of their objective of legitimizing their control over Tibet, since they recognized that the unique institution of the Dalai Lama meant they needed his consent. During the Sino-Tibetan negotiations, a constant Chinese concern was the possibility of flight by the Dalai Lama to India. The Chinese leadership, therefore, continued to keep India on its side. Despite the mutual bitterness and recrimination over the PLA's invasion at the end of 1950, Mao Zedong himself was the chief guest at India's first Republic Day celebration in January 1951. He was very cordial and made no reference to the unpleasantness between the two sides over Tibet. In March, Premier Zhou Enlai similarly engaged Ambassador Panikkar on the issue, taking him into confidence on the state of negotiations with Tibetan authorities and even suggesting that this was in conformity with India's advice. Zhou's real objective was to ensure that the Dalai Lama did not flee to India. He told Panikkar that some people were urging the Dalai Lama to leave for India, and that China wished the Dalai Lama to remain in Tibet so that the negotiations were settled in a mutually acceptable way. Zhou said that India's interests were that peace of her frontiers should not be disturbed, leading to unsettled conditions, and he hoped that the Government of India would not encourage the Dalai Lama to leave the country, or else it would bring a 'dark cloud between our good relations of friendship'. As a final sop, he gave another assurance to Panikkar that all Indian interests in Tibet could be safeguarded by negotiations.[16] India failed to recognize the deception and swallowed the Chinese bait again. India's Mission in Lhasa and the political officer in Gangtok were asked to discreetly convey to the Tibetans that the Dalai Lama should not be encouraged to seek asylum in India.[17]

The other concern of China, of external interference, centered on Nepal. Zhou Enlai probed Panikkar more than once whether the King (Tribhuvan), who had ousted the pro-British Ranas from power (with India's assistance), was susceptible to British or American influence, and might provide them with a staging ground to interfere in Tibet. This was a deep concern for China at the time. Chinese leader Liu Shaoqi confirmed this in his conversation with Soviet Ambassador Roshchin in May 1951, when he told him that Chinese plans to insert the PLA into Tibet would be complicated if Nepal interfered in the Tibetan question.[18] Nepal had historically invaded Tibet in previous centuries and this was, therefore, a matter of genuine concern for the Chinese. India was again quick to provide reassurance to the Chinese on this count. China's tactics in keeping India engaged over Tibet in 1951 without raising the points of contention, bought vital time and space for the Chinese to conclude the 17-Point Agreement between the Central Government of China and the Local Government of Tibet on Measures for the Peaceful Liberation of Tibet on 23 May 1951. With India having dissuaded the Dalai Lama from coming to India, he also eventually accepted the 17-Point Agreement on 24 October 1951. Thus, by the end of 1951, the Chinese had achieved the second phase of their strategy, namely to secure a legal basis for the People's Republic of China's claim over Tibet, and ended the possibility of united Tibetan opposition to Chinese rule.

India's strategy and tactics after the invasion in October–November 1950 was revealed by the Prime Minister in his note of 18 November 1950. India's policy in Tibet was to be determined by two factors: first, the need to look at Tibet in the larger context of relations with the People's Republic of China, which was now firmly entrenched in Beijing; and the recognition that India did not have the capacity or capability to assist Tibet to militarily resist a Chinese takeover.[19] These were reasonable presumptions, but the conclusion was that Tibet could not be saved and, therefore, the 'real protection we (India) should seek is some kind of understanding with China' that can help Tibet retain a large measure of autonomy.[20] Patel's advice had been to review the entire approach and to open discussions with China on problem areas, including the boundary, but this was not heeded. Instead, throughout 1950, India decided to keep its counsel, and to be helpful to the Chinese in the hope of earning goodwill. This might also explain the actions that India took with respect to Zhou Enlai's requests about not allowing the Dalai Lama to seek sanctuary in India and about dissuading Nepal from pursuing a military option in Tibet. These two tactical cards available to India were surrendered in the hope that it could convince China about its good intentions and help preserve a measure of Tibetan independence as well as its own interests in Tibet.

The 17-Point Agreement in May 1951 ought to have been another occasion for the Government of India to review its approach on the Tibet Question. But it had been decided that the Tibet issue would not be raised with China. Hence India foreclosed on the option of learning the implications for India about the Agreement directly from the Chinese. The 17-Point Agreement had been explicit in stating that Tibet was a part of China and that the Tibetan government was only a local government with no authority over its own foreign affairs and defence. India clutched at straws instead. It drew the inference from Clause 3 that Tibet would retain its autonomy, and from Clause 14 that Tibet would continue to have trade relations with neighbouring countries, without paying attention to the qualifying stipulation in both clauses that this would be under the overall direction and control of Beijing. The Indian side also overlooked the direct implications for India from a key stated objective in the very first clause of the Agreement, namely the elimination of 'imperialist aggressive forces' from Tibet.

The only 'imperialist' force present inside Tibet was India, and the Chinese media had referred to this on several occasions. India's failure to recognize this point meant that it did not conduct a fresh review of policy towards Tibet and China, in order to prepare for the possibility that China would bring up the issue of Indian presence in Tibet. Instead, two other presumptions appear to have been made. First, from Zhou's reassurance to Panikkar in very general terms about safeguarding India's interests in Tibet in March 1951 and the 17-Point Agreement of May 1951, India may have believed that the Chinese had achieved their objective and were not likely to question the frontier or India's special position in Tibet. Second, with the 17-Point Agreement in place, India may have thought there would no longer be good reason for the PLA to push further into Tibet or to be deployed along the India–Tibet frontier.

The presumptions were erroneous, but policy also dictated that Indian representatives should not unilaterally raise such issues with the Chinese side. Thus the possibility of getting some insight into the Chinese thinking on this matter or probing them on matters of India's concerns was also ruled out. In the several high-level interactions that Ambassador Panikkar had with the Chinese leaders in 1951, the subject of Tibet was never raised. On 20 November 1951, Nehru would inform the Indian Parliament that India's maps show that the McMahon Line is its boundary and it would remain so, map or no map.[21] The Chinese were able to spend 1951 consolidating their control over Tibet both legally and militarily, reasonably assured that India would not interfere in the process, and also having secured an assurance that Nepal territory would not be allowed to become a staging point for anti-Chinese activity in Tibet.

During this time, the Chinese were careful not to allow the PLA to come into direct contact with Indian forces along the frontier, or to agitate the existence of special privileges that India had in Tibet. When the Central Chinese Government's Representative in Lhasa, General Zhang Jingwu, raised the question of Indian interests in Tibet with his leadership, Premier Zhou Enlai sent him a message in September 1951, conveying that the time was not yet ripe for dealing with India on the issue.[22] By the end of 1951, therefore, China had achieved two of its objectives—physical control as well as the legitimization of its ownership of Tibet. Its next objective was to get India to recognize this fact. In 1952, China prepared to deal with Indian interests in Tibet.

When Panikkar raised the Tibet issue with Vice Foreign Minister Zhang Hanfu on 11 February 1952, and handed over a note on the subject, Zhang said he would pass it on to Premier Zhou Enlai. The note proposed a list of issues for discussion with the Chinese side relating to the special privileges that India had in Tibet by virtue of being the successor state to the British Indian

Government, with one notable exception—there was no reference to the frontier, which had now become the India–China frontier. By this time, the Indian side appeared to have drawn comfort from the absence of any mention by China about the boundary issue in the two years since the establishment of the People's Republic of China. It was felt that it was best to let the matter rest. On 13 February 1952, Panikkar met Zhou Enlai to discuss the note apropos Tibet that he had given to Vice Minister Zhang. Zhou's response was that China too desired to settle all issues through discussion, adding that 'we see no difficulty in safeguarding economic and cultural interests of India in Tibet'.[23] India had more than just economic and cultural relations with Tibet; it had a political relationship since it deemed Tibet to be autonomous. With regard to the note itself, Zhou confined himself to saying that he was studying it carefully and hoped to talk about it at an early date. No specific time-frame was mentioned. In fact, the Chinese took a full four months to reply to the Indian proposals. The delay in responding was tactical. These months were used for extensive research into Tibetan archives.

The delay also allowed the Chinese to complete the military occupation of Tibet. The PLA began to move southwards along the India–Tibet border. Premier Zhou Enlai informed the Central Chinese Government's Representative in Lhasa, General Zhang Jingwu, in February 1952 that the resolution of issues with India over Tibet would have to wait for the PLA to reach the southern boundary of Tibet. When India flagged its concerns in this regard, the Chinese dismissed them as provocative reports that were the creation of imperialists (the US and the UK) who were bent on spoiling the good relations between India and China. In reality, China was using the time to prepare the grounds for the next phase of its strategy. Zhou Enlai directed General Zhang Jingwu to ensure that negotiations with India should be preceded by the establishment of a Tibet Military

Committee and a Foreign Affairs Bureau fully controlled from Beijing, so that there was no reason for India to deal directly with the Tibetan government. Zhou also instructed the Chinese officials in Lhasa to conduct a detailed study of all materials in connection with India's privileges and rights in Tibet. In effect, the Chinese were engaged in doing two things in the first half of 1952 while India waited for a Chinese response to their proposal for a discussion on Tibet. They prepared thoroughly for the negotiation with India and they started to change the facts on the ground. By mid-1952, this was almost complete and Zhou was able to inform Josef Stalin that the question of whether there should be Chinese troops in Tibet was moot because they were already at the border with India.[24]

While India was waiting for the Chinese to respond to their proposal of 13 February 1952, the Indian Mission in Lhasa sent another valuable input in April. They reported to New Delhi that the Chinese had told the Tibetans that they would shortly take up with India the question of their relations with Tibet, including the Tibetan claims to areas like Ladakh and Tawang.[25] The Indian Mission also reported that the Chinese representatives in Lhasa had told the Tibetans that they were waiting for a favourable opportunity to regain these areas, and till that time, this issue would remain alive. This was a very important piece of information because it spoke of the extensive claims on Indian territory by China. In doing so, it questioned the very basis of two Indian presumptions: first, that China not raising doubts about the boundary with India meant that it had acquiesced in the alignment of the frontier; and second, that if India did not raise this issue, the Chinese might not raise it either. This latest information from Lhasa, on the contrary, suggested that the Chinese were aware of Tibetan claims with respect to the boundary and territory, and were preparing to call the India–Tibet frontier into question at an appropriate time. It ought to have, at the very least, re-opened the premise upon which the Government of India had worked, namely that Chinese silence on the issue of India's northern frontier was tantamount to acceptance, or at least acquiescence, of its current alignment.

Other developments reported by the Indian Mission in Lhasa were also noteworthy. Small incidents of an adverse nature against Indian interests in Tibet began to surface. In April 1952, Chinese troops obstructed the movement of Indian diplomatic pouches, opened the ordinary mail bags, and searched the baggage of Indian military officers. Then, on 10 May 1952, the Trade Agent in Gyantse reported that Captain Chibber, the Commanding Officer of the Indian Military Escort in Gyantse, had been physically stopped by Chinese troops and forced to dismount his horse under threat of the gun, despite him and his party being in uniform. General Zhang Jingwu dismissed these as inconsequential incidents of a local nature. These untoward incidents appeared to be challenging India's special privileges under the treaties signed between Great Britain and Tibet, and should have triggered a review. Instead, the Government of India continued to wait for a response to their proposal for talks contained in the note that Panikkar had handed over in February. Consultation and coordination between the headquarters (New Delhi) and the field (Indian Mission in Lhasa) was poor in comparison with the way in which the Chinese central government and its representatives in Lhasa were working to achieve their goals.

The Chinese response finally came on 15 June 1952, by which time China was well entrenched in Tibet and the instructions that Zhou had given to Zhang Jingwu in Lhasa had been substantially carried out. Premier Zhou Enlai felt that the preparations now allowed him to open a discussion with Panikkar on Tibet. He began by making a general statement that all the treaties between Great Britain and Tibet were unequal treaties that were forced upon Tibet and China through aggression, and that the Chinese government deemed these treaties and agreements to be no longer in existence. He hoped that India had no intention of claiming 'special rights' arising from these unequal treaties and would be prepared to negotiate a new relationship to safeguard legitimate interests of both parties.

Zhou framed this in terms of 'principle' and proposed that both sides first reach a consensus on this 'principle'. If India agreed to this principle, Zhou suggested that the first concrete issue to be resolved was the nature of the Lhasa Mission. He proposed that the Lhasa Mission be re-designated as a Consulate General, and that China be permitted to open a reciprocal office in Bombay (Mumbai). He added that all other matters like post and telegraph facilities, military escorts and trade marts were 'technical' issues that could be left for later negotiation because China did not want to create a vacuum in Tibet as a result of any changes to these arrangements. He never referred to the India–China (Tibet) boundary at all.[26]

On the face of it, the principle was unexceptionable and the change in nomenclature of Indian presence in Tibet appeared to be a matter of re-designation. It was, in fact, the nub of the discussion. The proposal would not only change the legal status of the Indian presence in Tibet, it would, as Zhou Enlai told Zhang Jingwu, end the old relationship between India and Tibet forever.[27] This was classic Chinese salami-slicing tactics. Zhou's proposals had serious implications for India. If the Chinese maintained, as a matter of principle, that all previous treaties were invalid and a new relationship had to be negotiated, then it automatically followed that the Simla Agreement of 1914 was also no longer valid and the McMahon Line was illegal. It blew the Indian argument that the McMahon Line was the final boundary between India and Tibet (now China) right out of the water.

Panikkar, however, pointed out that Zhou Enlai had not questioned the alignment of the frontier and strongly recommended that as the frontier had already been defined by India, there should be nothing more to discuss with the Chinese. Again, seemingly without much internal consultation, on 18 June 1952, Nehru concurred with Panikkar's line of thought on the boundary question, and also consented to Zhou's proposal for conversion of the Mission in Lhasa into a Consulate General without apparently realizing either its legal or its political implications.

After receiving India's written confirmation on the matter, the Chinese also quickly informed India that they had established an Assistant for Foreign Affairs in Lhasa (this had been Zhou's instruction to Zhang Jingwu), and that, henceforth, the new Indian Consulate General should deal with Tibet only through this new office. In accepting Zhou's proposals, India had agreed to three things. First, by accepting the principle that the earlier treaties were unequal, India had acquiesced in undermining the legal basis for all its privileges in Tibet as well as the Simla Agreement of 1914. Second, by converting the Lhasa Mission into a Consulate General and giving a reciprocal facility to China in Bombay, it had changed the status of its relationship with the Tibetan government from a political relationship to a consular one. By inference, this also meant that India had accepted that Tibet was a part of the People's Republic of China. And third, by agreeing to contact Tibetan authorities only through Chinese intermediaries in Lhasa, India had surrendered its right to have direct dealings with the Tibetan administration. This showed the methodical and practical nature of China's negotiating strategy and tactics; China had done serious research on the treaties and other materials in possession of the Tibetan government about Indian interests in Tibet, and devised a negotiating plan.

The Government of India, on the other hand, went about the negotiations in an ad hoc fashion and without adequate internal consultation, leave alone proper research on facts. There was good advice available on hand. After seeing the telegram from

Panikkar to Nehru, Sir G.S. Bajpai, the governor of Bombay (and former secretary general of the Ministry of External Affairs), wrote to Foreign Secretary N.R. Pillai on 14 July 1952, expressing concern that doubts would inevitably arise on the legitimacy of the frontier itself if India agreed with the principle proposed by Zhou Enlai. Bajpai also conveyed that 'this business of Sino-Indian relations over Tibet would, in my judgement, be best handled comprehensively and not piecemeal.'[28] Bajpai had hit upon the nub of the issue: the Chinese wanted to deal with India piecemeal or step-by-step, gradually advancing towards their final objective without raising undue alarm in India. Bajpai's advice appeared to go unheeded. Nehru and the Government of India were now locked in a self-generated belief that Zhou Enlai's silence on the frontier question was, in fact, tantamount to Chinese acquiescence in, if not acceptance of, India's position, since the Chinese had never raised doubts over the McMahon Line nor claimed areas beyond it. On 31 July 1952, New Delhi explicitly forbade the Indian Embassy in Beijing to raise the frontier question at all.

Bajpai made a second attempt, in his letter to Panikkar on 7 August 1952, to caution the Government of India against assuming that Chinese had tacitly accepted the frontier, pointing out that the Chinese had never accepted the McMahon Line as the frontier. This advice, too, went unheeded. Consequently, the Government of India set aside the boundary question, which was the one issue that mattered to India's national security, and focused its preparations on how it could defend the special privileges that India enjoyed in Tibet by virtue of the treaties between Great Britain and Tibet. It had not comprehended that its very acceptance of the principle that Zhou had proposed, of all such earlier treaties being unequal and non-existent, may have made the continuation of privileges arising from such treaties as moot. Accepting the Chinese proposal to re-designate the Indian Mission also eroded India's negotiating position since it accepted, by implication, that Tibet was not truly autonomous but a part of China. India's privileges became politically unviable and legally indefensible. India would go into the final negotiations in 1954 with a weak hand, having given up almost all the tactical advantages that it had held before 1950.

With the legal status of Tibet as part of China no longer in doubt after the 17-Point Agreement, with China having gained physical control over Tibet as far south as the Chumbi Valley and other areas along the India–China (Tibet) frontier, and with India having agreed to the principle that earlier treaties were no longer in existence, China unfolded the final leg of its strategy on Tibet. The Chinese had set two final tasks for themselves—to eliminate all historical privileges given to India and Nepal under the now defunct treaties, and to ensure that China's neighbours established normal ties with China by, presumably, accepting that Tibet was a part of China.[29] In line with these objectives, from late 1952, the Chinese started to apply pressure on India by protesting about certain activities by the Indian trade agents inside Tibet—for instance, alleging that they were distributing anti-China material—and through systematic harassment of Indian facilities and personnel. Their pressure focused, in particular, on the one area where India still held some advantage, its military escorts in Tibet. The Chinese began to accuse the Indian military personnel of bringing into Tibet a disproportionate number of guns that were beyond the legitimate needs of self-defence and in violation of international law. They hinted that this may be part of an arms smuggling operation to help the Tibetan resistance. They forcibly confiscated the wireless receiver and transmitter of the Trade Office in Gartok and blocked the Indian trade agent from freely moving to trade marts within Tibet. Finally, at the end of August 1953, they conveyed that China wanted India to withdraw its military escorts in Gyantse and Yadong and that it would not allow any relief military escorts to replace them. By August 1953, the Chinese were probably in a position to expel the

Indian military escorts from Gyantse and Yadong since the PLA was already deployed in sizeable numbers in the Chumbi Valley.

It went to the credit of Chinese strategic thinking and planning that they chose to persuade rather than compel India to withdraw. They understood that Indian goodwill was still needed to allow food and supplies to flow through Sikkim to the PLA in Tibet, since the supply routes from the East were still very limited. China also still needed India's cooperation in international affairs, including the Korean and Indo–China questions. Persuasion through engagement was seen by China as the desirable tactic in order to ensure that India 'may not be aggravated at the instigation of bad-willed nations'. This was also General Zhang Jingwu's advice to Zhou in October 1953, and it demonstrated how China took all factors into policy-making and allowed tactics to be determined accordingly.[30]

The pressure that China put on India inside Tibet worked. India began to press for negotiations. On 2 September 1953, Ambassador N. Raghavan conveyed Nehru's message to Zhou Enlai that the Government of India was cognizant of the new situation prevailing in Tibet and wanted to hold talks at the earliest opportunity to consider all pending matters relating to Tibet, in view of certain incidents that had affected the functioning of India's representatives. Zhou Enlai agreed to the proposal after he consulted Mao and other Chinese leaders. The necessary research had been completed and the ground realities had been changed, precisely as Zhou Enlai had advised Zhang Jingwu in February 1952. The Chinese suggested that if India were to voluntarily withdraw its military escorts from Gyantse and Yadong, it would be viewed as a positive step by India towards settlement of the question of relations between India and China in Tibet. This was the last leverage of any consequence that India had in Tibet. On 29 September 1953, India agreed in principle, 'as a gesture of goodwill and friendship'[31] to the withdrawal of all military escorts in Tibet. Yet another unilateral concession was obtained by China without bloodshed, prior to the commencement of the talks. It was only after India had made substantial unilateral concessions on India's legal, military and political presence in Tibet that China, finally in September 1953, agreed to talks with India on Tibet in Beijing in December 1953.

Zhang Jingwu, Zhang Guohua, Yang Gongsu and others who were given the responsibility by the Central Committee of the Communist Party of China were asked to meet the Dalai Lama and the members of the Kashag (Tibetan government) and to collate all the documents relating to India and Tibet that were in Tibetan possession. It is through the Kashag that the Chinese learned about the precise details of the negotiations between Tibet and India that had led to the Simla Agreement of 1914 and the finalization of the McMahon Line. They were shown the original text of the agreement, as well as the map on which the McMahon Line was drawn as a thick red line. They learned that there was no mutually agreed accompanying description of the delimited boundary line in the 1914 Agreement, nor a delimitation protocol. The British had not undertaken delimitation and demarcation before they departed from India in 1947. The Tibetans also told them about their claims on Ladakh, Darjeeling and Tawang which they had raised with the Government of India in 1947, and of how India was enforcing its claim south of the McMahon Line by extending civil administration and the army's presence, especially in Tawang. These documents enabled the Chinese to gradually comprehend the complexity of the boundary issue with India. As one of the Chinese representatives, Yang Gongsu, put it, 'This was the first time we saw the real picture.'[32] The Central Committee of the Communist Party of China set up an eleven-member committee consisting of representatives from the central government, the Tibetan local government and the PLA to guide the negotiators.[33] It was during a meeting of this Committee that

Zhou Enlai decided that it would be better not to discuss the boundary issue with India since matters were yet unclear. He said that the discussion should be limited to issues that were mature for settlement.

India's preparation, in contrast with China's, left much to be desired. A detailed review of the happenings since 1950, and especially the implications of concessions made by India, on the legality of its rights and privileges in Tibet, were not examined. Information provided by the Consul General in Lhasa and the Political Officer in Gangtok were filed away. In one case, in late 1953, when Consul General S. Sinha wrote of the imminent danger to India as a result of 'Chinese designs on the north-eastern frontier', he was reprimanded by the Government of India for having fanciful ideas. Nehru recorded the following minute: 'It appears that Mr Sinha does not appreciate our policy fully. He should be enlightened.'[34] Ignoring inputs from Lhasa that the Chinese were studying all documents relating to the India–China boundary in Tibet, a policy note from the prime minister on 3 December 1953 decided once and for all that the question of the frontier would not be raised or discussed during the forthcoming India–China talks about Tibet, because it was already a settled issue.[35] India wanted a limited discussion on the facilities it enjoyed in Tibet.

The talks began in Beijing on 31 December 1953 with a meeting between the Indian delegation led by T.N. Kaul and Premier Zhou Enlai. Here Zhou reiterated that outstanding issues could be solved only on the basis of mutual respect for sovereignty and territorial integrity; in other words, it could not be decided on the basis of unequal treaties that Great Britain had forced upon Tibet or China. But even more significantly, Zhou said that only those questions would be taken up for discussion that 'are ripe for settlement'.[36] These were carefully chosen words. In the course of their systematic research, they began to understand the complexity of the boundary issue as well as the Indian thinking. In October

1953, the Chinese central government's representative in Lhasa, General Zhang Jingwu, opined that India 'claimed the absence of territorial disputes just to force us into implicitly acknowledging and legitimizing their occupation. We must stay alert in this regard.' His advice was to delay the settlement of the border issue, but to engage India on all other matters relating to Tibet since India's cooperation was desirable for China in international affairs.[37] The Chinese devised their strategy accordingly, and decided not to bring the McMahon Line into the ambit of the discussion since it was not 'ripe for settlement'. This was an excellent example of how China would adjust its strategy and tactics on the basis of facts. India had already presumed that Chinese silence on the matter meant acceptance of the current reality, and the fact that China never raised this issue in the 1954 negotiations only served to convert the presumption into incontrovertible fact. It would prove fatal for India.

In the talks, China's strategy was to secure the full, final and unambiguous acknowledgement from India about Tibet as a part of China; to end all special privileges for India in Tibet; and to put off any discussion about the frontier until a later date. This had already been substantially achieved on the ground, but China wanted it to be agreed upon bilaterally, in the form of a treaty. China's tactic in the first three days of discussion was to draw the Indian side out fully on all the issues, in order to comprehend the Indian position and expectations in detail. The Chinese chief negotiator, Vice Foreign Minister Zhang Hanfu, listened and took notes, while the Indian delegation, as Ambassador Raghavan subsequently wrote to Nehru, put 'all our cards on the table'.[38]

The Chinese sought the minutest details while reserving their views. After three days of talks, when they had extracted the full details of the Indian position, the Chinese shifted gears by suggesting that both sides first reach common agreement on some basic principles, including mutual respect for sovereignty and territorial integrity and non-use of force (it would later become the Five Principles of Peaceful Co-existence). The objective was to give legal sanctity to something that India had already agreed to, the principle that the unequal treaties upon which Indian claims to privileges in Tibet were based, were violative of Chinese sovereignty and territorial integrity. India agreed. After securing India's acquiescence to these principles, the Chinese proceeded to whittle away at the Indian position on all the specific issues. They stood firm on the withdrawal of the military escort; on the ending of special rights to India to have its own post and telegraph facilities and rest houses; on special jurisdiction for Indian trade agents in certain situations; and that Indians could have dealings with the Tibetans only through Chinese Foreign Affairs Bureaus in Gyantse and Yadong, and not directly. While the Chinese dragged on the talks through February and March 1954, pressure was also subtly generated through continued movement of PLA troops to the frontline, and by spreading propaganda within the Tibetan population that China was planning to expel India from Tibet, in order to create panic among the Tibetan population.

India brought more pressure on itself by becoming anxious about concluding a settlement before the Geneva Conference began in May 1954. Again, the primary consideration for this was not national security but India's international image. Nehru wrote to Raghavan on 16 April 1954 to urge him to close the deal, saying, 'If the Indo-Chinese Agreement on Tibet is signed and announced soon it will have salutary effect. If, however, this is postponed indefinitely, this will have contrary effect . . . This will create impression of failure which will not be good.'[39] By stretching out the negotiations, China thus managed to get India to give up even the lesser demands. In a final act of misplaced magnanimity, India ultimately even waived off the financial compensation that China had agreed to pay in return for the turning over of Indian post and telegraph facilities, guest houses and vacant land in Gyantse, Yadong and Lhasa by India to the Chinese side. The four-year Chinese effort was a complete vindication of China's strategy and negotiating abilities.

In a note recorded post-facto, Indian chief negotiator T.N. Kaul justified giving up most of the special privileges on the grounds that in the 1908 Trade Agreement with Tibet, the British Indian Government had already agreed to return them to Tibet when it was ready to assume the responsibility of governing itself.[40] Kaul conveniently side-stepped the fact that China, in any case, had annulled all earlier treaties, and that being the case, India was not obliged to comply with any of its provisions. Kaul also claimed that India had benefitted from the new trade agreement with China, and he listed the recognition of the boundary, by implication, as one such important gain. This claim was made because China had named six border passes in the Middle Sector for purposes of conducting trade between India and Tibet, which, according to the Indian side, by implication meant that China had no quarrel over the alignment of the India–Tibet boundary line along its entire length. Dr Gopalachari, who was also a member of the Indian delegation, reportedly wrote a dissenting note cautioning the Government of India against this assumption that China had accepted the frontier as defined by India,[41] but his advice was ignored as it did not fit into the Government's framework. In the euphoria that the Agreement generated, which Nehru described as 'a new starting point for our relations with China and Tibet', he also directed that 'all our old maps dealing with this frontier should be carefully examined and where necessary withdrawn. New maps should be printed showing our northern and north-eastern frontier without any reference to any line (McMahon) . . . Both as flowing from our policy and as a consequence of our agreement with China, this frontier should be considered a firm and definite one which is not open to discussion with anybody.'[42]

The Government of India now locked itself into a straitjacket on the boundary question.

In the 1954 diplomatic negotiations, the Chinese had clear objectives—the exercise of de jure sovereignty over Tibet and the ending of all historical extra-territorial (India) influence. The core objectives were achieved systematically one step at a time. It first 'liberated' Tibet in 1950 by marching in the PLA; then it consolidated its position on the ground by reaching a political agreement with Tibetans (17-Point Agreement) and militarily occupying all the territory. In the first two phases, China's strategy was to keep India on its side in order that it did not join the American anti-Communist efforts or provide assistance to the Tibetan government or resistance movements. Deception and engagement were some of the tactics used by them. They bought time to consolidate their control and to prepare for negotiations. At each stage, the Chinese probed the Indian thinking, including in several conversations between Premier Zhou Enlai and Indian Ambassador Panikkar. They engaged in careful study and research.

Based on these inputs they decided to deal with India in a piecemeal fashion rather than in a comprehensive way. When the facts showed that the boundary issue was complex, the Chinese decided to put it aside and to allow a temporary status quo to prevail; although, in their minds, India was in occupation of Chinese territory. In overall terms, their strategy resulted, in April 1954, in cancellation of all special privileges and rights that India enjoyed in Tibet, and securing, in a legally binding way, India's consent to China's occupation of Tibet by recognizing it as a 'Region' of China. In the end, all that was left of a complex problem in 1950 was an unresolved boundary issue, for which the Chinese had bought time and Indian goodwill until they were ready to deal with India from a position of strength.

III

Pokhran: How to Untie a
Knot from the Tiger's Neck

Our nuclear *pas de deux* with the Chinese began several decades before India conducted five nuclear tests at Pokhran in the Rajasthan desert in May 1998.

Mao's desire to have a nuclear bomb was not a secret. In April 1956, Mao Zedong had told an enlarged meeting of the Politburo that 'in today's world if we don't want to be bullied, we have to have this thing (nuclear bomb)'.[1] By September 1960, when it had become amply clear to the Chinese Communists, especially following a conversation between Soviet ideologue Mikhail Suslov and Deng Xiaoping, that the Soviets had no intention of assisting the Chinese nuclear programme,[2] Mao decided to go it alone. He secured the services of Qian Xuesen, a Chinese scientist who had studied in America and gone on to be a part of the Manhattan Project (the US nuclear weapons experimental project during the Second World War). Qian was, thus, uniquely placed to steer the Chinese nuclear programme when he returned to the country after being accused of Communist sympathies during the McCarthy era of the 1950s. By 1963, it was a question of not if, but when, China would test its atomic bomb.

The Government of India was also preparing for this day. In August 1963, Homi Bhabha, the chairman of India's Atomic Energy Commission, had offered advice to Prime Minister Nehru on what India should do in the light of the psychological and political impact that a Chinese nuclear test might have in terms of the balance of power in Asia. Bhabha correctly assessed that such a test may not pose an immediate military threat to India, but the psychological fallout could be catastrophic for a nation that was still reeling from the aftermath of a border war with China in 1962. Bhabha wrote: 'I am inclined to the view that the only way this can be done at present is for us to show that, should China explode such a device, we are in a position to do so within a few months thereafter.'[3] From the very beginning, China was an important consideration in our nuclear calculations.

The first Chinese nuclear test was conducted at Lop Nor on 16 October 1964. Chinese Premier Zhou Enlai wrote to heads of state and government, including Prime Minister Lal Bahadur Shastri (Nehru had passed away in May 1964). As might be expected, the letter contained China's justification for the nuclear test, which Premier Zhou said China was 'compelled' to conduct in order to protect the Chinese people from the US nuclear threat. Zhou's letter also contained a proposal to convene an international conference to 'reach an agreement to the effect the nuclear powers and those countries which may soon become nuclear powers undertake not to use nuclear weapons . . .'[4] It was an interesting formulation, that hinted at the possibility that they knew that India might also have been developing such capabilities. If this was an attempt to build a common front in the Third World, then India either missed the signal or chose to ignore it. Describing the Chinese tests as 'retrograde and deplorable',[5] Shastri rejected the Chinese explanation, saying the Chinese action placed 'serious obstacles' towards the elimination of nuclear weapons. Perhaps a chance was lost, although in retrospect it is not clear whether the Chinese were serious about this idea.

The Chinese expected us to test our own nuclear device sooner or later. In June 1971, Zhou told Romanian President Nicolae Ceausescu that 'as far as the production of the atom bomb is concerned, probably India wants to create an equilibrium in its relations with China'.[6] When India tested its nuclear device in May 1974, the Chinese statement, issued on 19 May 1974, was, therefore, factual. More intriguingly, there were no public references to India's test when Pakistan's Foreign Minister, Agha Shahi, came visiting China from 6 to 10 June 1974. In private, however, the Chinese were dismissive. Japan's Prince Saiyonji reported Vice Premier Deng Xiaoping as telling him that India's nuclear test was not likely to help raise India's prestige in the world.[7] The Chinese were careful not to link India's nuclear test to the Chinese tests. This was a calculated move. They did not wish to give any opportunity for India to be equated with them. Hence, the two commentaries in *People's Daily* on the subject of India's nuclear tests, on 28 June and 3 September 1974, described India as a 'sub-super power' intent on 'nuclear blackmail and nuclear menace in the South Asia region'. There was no reference to the impact of India's test either in the larger Asian context or the global context.

China had, presumably, already begun to help Pakistan with its nuclear programme. In November 1974, when US Secretary of State Henry Kissinger met with Vice Premier Deng Xiaoping in Beijing, he casually dropped a bait by telling Deng that the head of his policy planning staff, Winston Lord (later the American Ambassador to China in the 1980s), had been in favour of giving nuclear weapons to Pakistan.[8] The Americans had already guessed that China was assisting Pakistan, and Kissinger was seeking affirmation from the Chinese. Deng did not rise to the bait. Silence was invariably used as a tactic whenever the

Chinese did not wish to address any matter. This also allowed for deniability about China's involvement in Pakistan's nuclear programme. When Prime Ministers Rajiv Gandhi and Narasimha Rao would subsequently raise the supply by China to Pakistan of M-11 nuclear-capable missiles and ring magnets for centrifuges with Chinese leaders, there would be the same studied silence, the same denials.

China had stayed outside the Nuclear Non-Proliferation Treaty's (NPT) ambit through the 1970s. However, in the 1980s, under Deng Xiaoping, China had begun to 'normalize' its dealings with the outside world. Deng's Modernization Programme needed both external financing and a stable geo-strategic environment, and he introduced consequent changes in how China dealt with the world.[9] On 17 March 1992, therefore, China formally acceded to the NPT. In 1995, during the NPT Review Conference, China gained first-hand experience in collaborating with the N-5 (five nuclear weapon states recognized in the NPT) as a group, and realized the benefits in terms of global influence as a result of being a member of such an exclusive club. It joined the other nuclear weapons states in supporting an indefinite extension of the NPT. This was in sharp contrast to what Deng Xiaoping had told Indian journalists in Beijing after meeting Foreign Minister Atal Bihari Vajpayee in February 1979, namely that the nuclear powers had no right to ask other countries not to have nuclear weapons when the nuclear weapons states were not committing to eliminate their own nuclear weapons.[10] China had travelled a long way in just fifteen years.

Immediately thereafter, China enthusiastically participated in the negotiations on the Comprehensive Test Ban Treaty (CTBT). China was well aware that there were three threshold countries, but only one, India, represented a concern for them. Seeing a once-in-a-lifetime opportunity to permanently cripple the Indian nuclear programme, China played its part in ensuring that India's concerns over the CTBT were kept outside the purview of consultations. China's Ambassador for Disarmament, Sha Zukang, later said that there were no negotiations with India because it was none of their business. India, he said, chose to keep a distance. However, China also saw to it that, officially, there were no mechanisms or arrangements for the nuclear weapons states to understand India's position.[11] The outcome of the CTBT negotiations represented a triumph for China. It placed her firmly inside the nuclear club, aligned to the Americans and other nuclear-weapon states, and kept India outside, without the possibility of future nuclear assistance from any of the nuclear powers. China presumed that it had closed the loop as it were; they did not expect India to politically defy the international community.

When India tested three nuclear devices in Pokhran on 11 May 1998, the initial Chinese reaction was muted. They expressed 'grave concern' and proclaimed that India's nuclear testing 'runs against the international trend'.[12] After the second set of tests on 13 May, though, the Chinese response was very sharp. Their statement used strong language like 'deeply shocked' and 'strong condemnation'. China also urged the international community to adopt a common position in demanding that India stop further development of nuclear weapons. The clue to this drastic change in the Chinese stance came towards the very end of their statement, which said, 'It has maliciously accused China of posing a nuclear threat to India. This is utterly groundless.'[13] They had of course, by then, seen the letter—deliberately leaked by the Americans—from Prime Minister Atal Bihari Vajpayee to President Bill Clinton justifying the nuclear tests in terms of the nuclear threat in our periphery. Vajpayee had made a direct reference to the distrust that existed between India and China, as well as to the material assistance that China had rendered to Pakistan in its nuclear weapons programme. The Indian Prime Minister held China as one of the parties responsible for the deteriorating security environment in South Asia.[14]

The Indian narrative ran contrary to the narrative that China was crafting. By 1998, the Chinese were assiduously cultivating the image of a benign Great Power that was helping the world by developing itself and acting responsibly in terms of peace and security in the global context. They wanted to erase memories of the early years when China was perceived as a threat in the region. The justification that India was now offering in support of its nuclear tests threatened to undo this effort and revive the notion of the 'China Threat'. The *Liberation Army Daily*, which is the mouthpiece of the Chinese Army, proclaimed that India was raising a hue and cry about the 'China Threat' theory to land China in a difficult position in its (India) efforts to seek hegemony in South Asia.[15] China was angry because it felt that its image was being impugned.

The Indian nuclear tests had also caught the Chinese by complete surprise for two reasons. First, they regarded themselves as having a sound understanding of India's leadership and foreign policy, and assumed that India lacked the political will to challenge the international community on the nuclear issue. Second, their experience at the NPT Review Conference and the CTBT negotiations had imbued them with a sense of confidence that they had closed ranks with the United States of America and that both shared the common objective of enforcing the global nuclear non-proliferation arrangements without any exceptions. The Chinese presumed that India would not dare to go against the collective decision of the N-5. Therefore, they struggled to comprehend the new situation created by the Indian nuclear tests. Their broad assessment was that India was attempting to squeeze into the ranks of the nuclear states without caring for the price in terms of worsening India–China relations.

A well-known Chinese strategic expert alleged that there was a strong domestic motivation behind these nuclear tests, that the tests helped the ruling Bharatiya Janata Party (BJP) to consolidate its grip on power by talking up an external threat.[16] They surmised that the BJP wanted to exploit fault-lines between China and America in order to break apart the international coalition against India's nuclear tests. Despite the substantial improvement in Sino-US relations by the late 1990s (by which time they had repaired the damage caused to the relationship by the fallout from the Tiananmen incident of 1989), the Chinese were concerned about the prospects of being 'contained' by the United States. The presumption may have been that the nuclear tests would have strengthened India's position as a 'containing factor' for the Americans against China.[17] Hence, China's two primary questions immediately after the nuclear tests were: What would the Americans do next in terms of dealing with India's nuclear tests?; and, how could China protect her international image from the damage arising as a result of Indian accusations that China was a threat?

The Americans had also been caught by surprise by the Indian nuclear tests, which was all the greater because the Clinton administration had discovered and pre-empted an earlier effort during the administration of Prime Minister P.V. Narasimha Rao to test nuclear devices in December 1995.[18] The Chinese would have been relieved when President Clinton reacted strongly to news of the tests. Avowing that 'India has done the wrong thing. They are on the wrong side of history',[19] Clinton announced the imposition of economic sanctions on India. From the testimonies of responsible US officials before the United States Congressional Committee for South Asia on 13 May 1998, the Chinese may have figured that the American unhappiness was the consequence of the perceived setback to the process of securing Congressional ratification for the CTBT because of the Indian, and also possibly Pakistani, tests. The tests undermined the freeze-cap-rollback policy of the Clinton administration, and the CTBT that was a key achievement of Clinton's foreign policy. It was already facing pushback in the Senate. China likely worked on the presumption that the US would be very keen to stop Pakistan from following India, which might increase the value of China to the Americans. Their impression was confirmed when Clinton used the Hot Line for the first time ever to talk to China's leader, Jiang Zemin, about nuclear developments in South Asia.[20] China might have felt reassured by the strong American reaction to India's tests, and formulated its response accordingly. One of the hallmarks of Chinese diplomatic practice is that they rarely react impulsively. It helps when there is no free media or a watchful political opposition, but that is not the whole explanation. The decision-making process in China is deliberative, and at the official level (Ministries of Foreign Affairs, National Defence, State Security, etc.), it also pulls in the strategic community's inputs and weighs the global responses before the matter goes up the political chain of command for a decision. As a result, China's response time is longer. The Chinese, after full consideration, identified two major objectives: to punish India, and to rectify the damage that India had done to China's image. It developed its larger diplomatic strategy around these objectives.

The core of China's strategy revolved around how they could utilize the situation to isolate India to the greatest degree. Foremost in their thinking was their assessment that the Americans would have to be the key to uniting all the major powers in sanctioning India. China decided to make itself useful to the Americans, both in building an international coalition against India, and on interceding with Pakistan. The latter was tricky. China did not want to pressure Pakistan, or be subsequently held responsible for Pakistan's nuclear tests. The crucial element was proper coordination with the Americans. It helped that the Americans reached out to the Chinese for cooperation. The Clinton administration initially decided to turn a blind eye to the reasons adduced by India for conducting the tests. Testifying before the

Congressional Subcommittee on Near Eastern and South Asian Affairs, which was chaired by Senator Sam Brownback, on 13 May 1998, Assistant Secretary of State for South Asia Karl Inderfurth peremptorily rejected the Indian rationale about the China threat. His testimony to Congress focused on India's wanton repudiation of efforts by the international community to contain the spread of nuclear weapons.[21] Three weeks later, on 3 June, on the eve of a major meeting of the Foreign Ministers of the P-5 in Geneva to discuss the nuclear situation in South Asia, and again testifying before the same subcommittee, Inderfurth made a reference to the positive role of China. He said, 'We believe that it has been playing a more constructive role in non-proliferation issues of late. China is the coordinator of the P-5 for this (Geneva) meeting, and so the Secretary (Madeleine Albright) has been working directly with her counterpart, Foreign Minister Tang (Tang Jiaxuan) to see this meeting come about in a hopefully constructive and positive way.'[22] Such statements further validated the Chinese presumption that America was the key to building the international coalition that would punish India. It set about acting as the main coordinator behind the scenes, to unite the P-5. It followed the American lead throughout and allowed them to take all the credit. The Chinese efforts to build an international coalition also allowed it to disappear into the crowd. This is a classic diplomatic ruse known as 'Murder with a Borrowed Knife' (*Jie Dao Sha Ren*, a Chinese saying that basically meant shooting off another's shoulders). Inducing others to fight in its stead, in this case America, allowed China to achieve its objective without being at the forefront themselves. This stratagem could also prove useful to subsequently aver that it was someone else's fault if things did not proceed according to plan.

The meeting of the foreign ministers of the five Permanent Members of the UN Security Council (known as P-5) in Geneva, on 4 June 1998, went as per the diplomatic strategy that China had planned. The P-5 laid down five conditions for the lifting of sanctions on India (and Pakistan), namely that both had to sign the CTBT, join in negotiations for a Fissile Material Cut-off Treaty (FMCT), accept a strategic restraint regime on ballistic missiles, agree to tighter export controls on dual-use items, and to resume dialogue on Jammu and Kashmir. Sheltering behind the UN Security Council made it convenient, and also easier, for China to explain why it had agreed to economic sanctions when China's publicly stated position was that economic sanctions were neither acceptable nor effective. China also played up US and Western concerns about a possible nuclear war in South Asia over Kashmir as a consequence of the nuclear weaponization of India. In this whole effort, the Chinese took special care to make sure the United States always stayed in the limelight as the leader, but, as Michael Krepon put it, 'Beijing's imprint on the P-5's conditions was difficult to miss, as the proposed strategic restraint regime and FMCT would significantly constrain India from countering China's strategic modernization programmes.'[23] Krepon's assessment subsequently proved to be accurate. Sha Zukang, China's Ambassador to the Conference on Disarmament and later their Director General for Disarmament matters, implied as much in an oral interview that the Wilson Center recorded with him in 2016.[24] The references in the P-5 statement to the 'root causes' of tension between India and Pakistan in relation to the Kashmir question in particular, was the unkindest cut of all, and China was well aware when it proposed that language that they would be wounding India. The words 'root causes' are used by Pakistan to suggest that the main concern with regard to Kashmir is not terrorism (as India claims) but the unfinished agenda of Partition (as Pakistan claims). Hence, 'root causes', when used in the international context in a UN document, would give Pakistan's narrative on Kashmir a boost. China made sure that this language found its way into UN Security Resolution 1172 of 8 June 1998.[25]

The high point of success for China's strategy to punish India was the Clinton-Jiang Zemin Summit meeting on 27 June 1998. The two leaders issued a stand-alone Joint Statement on South Asia, which was by and in itself not acceptable to India. Matters were made worse by the wording of the document, which suggested that the Americans were giving the Chinese a central role in the maintenance of peace and stability in South Asia. Clinton had already publicly acknowledged such a role for China, during his remarks to the White House Press Corps in the White House Rose Garden on 3 June.[26] India viewed this as an overt manifestation of American alignment with China against India, somewhat akin to Nixon's 1972 tilt to China. It was a low point for the Indo–US relationship. One of its consequences was the absence of any meaningful contact between the embassies of the two countries in Beijing and in the shunning of Indian diplomats at the annual Fourth of July reception that was hosted by Jim Sasser, the US Ambassador to China on 3 July 1998.

It was at this point that the Chinese may have made their first mistake. They assumed that the Americans would follow through on their strategy of thoroughly punishing India. In reality, Deputy Secretary Strobe Talbott had been tasked by President Clinton to open discussions with Jaswant Singh, a senior member of the National Democratic Alliance Government. The Chinese did not appear to get wind of this until much later. The Vajpayee letter that the Clinton administration had leaked, had been drafted carefully. Prior to this, Vajpayee's team had made their own assessment about the Americans and concluded that the initial US response to the nuclear tests by India would not be the final American position. Vajpayee had personally probed American Ambassador Frank Wisner in August 1996 to get his sense about the possible implications for India if it went ahead with the tests.[27] BJP leaders, although not in office for long, had been in politics for decades and understood well the nuances of international politics.

The Indian side chose elements from the Chinese playbook in 1964 in order to blunt the Chinese case against them. China had also referred to the existence of a nuclear threat (from the US in their case) and of the transfer of nuclear weapons into the hands of another (to the West German 'revanchists', as Xinhua put it in its statement of 16 October 1964) to build their case. The Indian side also correctly assessed that the nuclear tests would pose a dilemma to the United States.

On the one hand, a weak US response to India's tests could challenge the US-led global nuclear non-proliferation efforts, while on the other hand a harsher response might disrupt Clinton's plans to strengthen ties with India. Hence Clinton, while imposing sanctions, also proposed bilateral engagement on the nuclear issue. Vajpayee responded positively to Clinton's proposal for discussions and appointed Jaswant Singh to negotiate. Strobe Talbott, the American negotiator, was to recall that he met Jaswant Singh fourteen times at ten locations in seven countries on three continents.[28] There was no one better than Singh to engage the Americans in a didactic discussion on the matter. Jaswant Singh, in his memoirs, later said that he was well aware that Clinton had less than three years left in his second term, and that he leveraged this time constraint to extract India from the sanctions (although this process was completed only during the Bush administration that followed) without conceding the core positions on the NPT and the CTBT.[29]

In the meantime, by the time the third hearing on India's nuclear tests took place in the US Congress on 13 July 1998, the Indian narrative was also beginning to resonate in other quarters in Washington, most notably on Capitol Hill (the earlier hearings had taken place on 13 May and 3 June). Indian Ambassador Naresh Chandra assiduously worked both sides of the Congressional aisle, and also roped in diplomatic seers such as Henry Kissinger by pushing the argument that in the long-term geo-political context,

India's nuclear tests were good for the United States. Naresh Chandra's diplomatic efforts proved critical to India's strategy in Washington. This gave an opportunity for the Republicans, then in Opposition, to put space between themselves and the Democratic Party on the nuclear issue. Talbott also acknowledged the difficulties that the Clinton administration faced in maintaining firm Congressional support for a tough India policy given the pro-Indian sentiment in both parties on Capitol Hill.[30] In the third meeting on the Hill on 13 July, Senator Sam Brownback pointedly asked Assistant Secretary Inderfurth about the Indian security concerns regarding China, which he had so blithely swatted away during his initial testimony on 13 May. Brownback averred that he and his colleague, Senator Charles S. Robb, had got an earful from Indian officials about the Jiang–Clinton Joint Statement on South Asia and the perceived US lack of sensitivity towards India's security concerns about China. This prompted Inderfurth to reverse his position: 'We do not believe nor have we stated that China should serve as a mediator in South Asian security matters.' Inderfurth also claimed in his testimony that the Americans had been able to secure a Chinese commitment to engage with India, but later admitted that they had 'listened very carefully to what we had to say'[31] without giving any firm commitment to talk to India.

In fact, the Chinese were doing precisely the opposite of what Inderfurth had claimed. They stepped up their efforts to keep India isolated and under international pressure. This is where the Chinese possibly might have committed another error of judgement with regard to their understanding of US policy. Their successful working relationship with the Americans during the NPT Review in 1995 and the CTBT negotiations in 1996 may, perhaps, have led them to think that the issue of non-proliferation was so important to the Americans that they would not waver in punishing India. In truth, a certain contempt for India had crept into Chinese thinking. This might have led them to overlook the fact that although India, by conducting the nuclear tests, had upset the American cart on non-proliferation matters, it still mattered for Clinton in terms of resuscitating the democratic partnership and in facilitating American entry into the Indian market. The Chinese possibly assumed that India would never be an attractive alternative to the Chinese in Asia, and this assumption led to a misreading of US policy post the Clinton–Jiang Zemin Summit.

So far as the Chinese handling of India was concerned, it was based on two assumptions. First, that the economic sanctions would make things increasingly difficult for India and force them to the negotiating table. Second, that by directing the 'spearhead' against the BJP, they could use domestic opposition to the nuclear tests to weaken the Indian leadership's hand. Having pushed their 'asks' through a collective decision of the UN Security Council in June 1998, and established their *locus standi* in South Asia via the Clinton–Jiang Zemin Joint Statement of 27 June 1998, the Chinese presumed that the Indians would likely buckle to the demands, and the US would stand firm.

It was on these presumptions that they crafted their policy of building pressure on India. The policy was one of deliberate 'cooling and isolation' in terms of contacts. China insisted that they were the aggrieved party and had been slandered by India. They used the Chinese proverb 'whoever has tied the knot on the tiger's neck must untie it' (*jie ling xi ling*), to suggest that it was for India to make unilateral reparations by, metaphorically, untying the knot they had tied. This was the Chinese way of laying down pre-conditions for India to fulfil before the restoration of normality in the bilateral relationship. As if on cue, the legion of Chinese 'academics' came out to justify the 'party line', including veteran India-watchers Ye Zhengjia and Wang Hongwei, both scholars of 1960s vintage, who harped on the Indian perfidy in dragging China's name into the matter and thus creating a new obstacle for the development of India–China relations. Given the paucity of direct access in China to decision-makers by foreign diplomats, most embassies carefully parsed academic writings from key Chinese think tanks affiliated to the Party and the government. The Chinese, therefore, knew that Indians would get the message that China expected them to kowtow, and to make amends for falsely accusing the Chinese of being a 'threat', if the bilateral relationship was to return to the normal track.

The problem was that the Chinese Communist Party and government did not have a proper measure of India. Chinese scholarship on India had languished after 1989, when China turned its academic focus to the West and other more profitable markets. After the end of the Cold War, India fell further down in the foreign policy priorities of China. As a result, by the late 1990s, the majority of Chinese experts on India were of 1960s vintage, and therefore out of touch with new developments in India. There was no proper assessment of the positive impact of the 1991 economic reforms on the Indian economy and the new resilience it had gained since then. The general impression of India among Chinese scholars was that of a country with a hobbled economy and a divided society. The economic crisis of 1990, the Mandal agitation, the assassination of Prime Minister Rajiv Gandhi and the terrorism in Jammu and Kashmir all fed into this Chinese narrative.* Their expectations that the Indian economy would

---

* 'I feel that China's relations with many of its neighbours, such as Vietnam, Mongolia and India are very complicated and changeable. But Chinese scholars have done little to research the history of these relations. Scholars and policymakers know little about the neighbourhood. I believe that historians should be held responsible for this inability to provide policymakers with the relevant background knowledge.'—H-Diplo Essay 267—Shen Zhihua, in the series Learning the Scholar's Craft: Reflections of Historians and International Relations Scholars, 15 September 2020, https://hdiplo.or/to/E267. Shen is Professor of History and Director of the Centre for Cold War International History Studies, East China Normal University, Shanghai, and a pre-eminent scholar of Cold War history in China.

collapse under the weight of international sanctions was, therefore, misplaced.

Similarly, the Chinese Communist leadership had little understanding of the new political leadership in India. The International Department of the Chinese Communist Party was created for precisely the purpose of building a parallel channel of communication with world leaders, but the Chinese had grown comfortable in dealing only with certain political families in South Asia. They did not make a proper effort to reach out to other political forces in India, and they also made the error of transposing their impressions of how the Congress Party conducted its foreign policy on to subsequent non-Congress governments. As a consequence, they had no real political understanding of the BJP or its thinking. A lopsided impression of India, captured in a cartoon in the *China Daily* of 21 April 1999, nearly a year after the nuclear tests, showed the BJP falling flat on their backs and looking disoriented after launching a nuclear bomb, as if to suggest that Vajpayee and his government did not know what they were doing. The disproportionate dependence of the Chinese on the Left parties in India, with whom the Chinese embassy in New Delhi maintained regular liaison, also influenced their thinking. The Chinese may have thought that the Left had not been as enthusiastic as the rest of the political spectrum about the nuclear tests. The Chinese possibly presumed that the internal political differences might be utilized to influence the direction of India's policy towards China in the post-May 1998 situation. Since their understanding about India was not up to date, the Chinese policy of 'cooling and isolation' could not achieve the desired outcomes. As a result, the Chinese were unable to exploit domestic differences while, at the international level, the ring-fence that the Chinese had tried to create through a unified P-5 stand and the UNSC Resolution 1172 also began to rupture as Indian diplomacy started to work.

India's efforts with the Americans began to show progress. Indian negotiators played on American pragmatism to get them to adjust to the new reality while holding out unspecified assurances of meeting benchmarks set by them on nuclear non-proliferation. In his recollection of the events in the summer of 1998, Michael Krepon has written on how Jaswant Singh kept the ball in play with the Americans with private assurances, without ever vocalizing them in public.[32] Strobe Talbott subsequently acknowledged this in his own book saying, 'Its [India's] strategy was to play for the day that the United States would get over its huffing and puffing and, with a sigh of exhaustion or a shrug of resignation, accept a nuclear armed India as a fully responsible and fully entitled member of the international community.'[33] India also judged—correctly as it turned out—that if it remained steadfast long enough to get the US to shift its position, it would only be a matter of time before the Chinese were also compelled to change course. Indian diplomatic strategy was, therefore, crafted in such a way as to be flexible with the Americans and unwavering with the Chinese. In hindsight, this was to prove the correct diplomatic strategy.

In order to prepare for that eventuality, the Indian Government began to tactically engage with China. This was deliberate policy in order to create the impression among the international community that India was ready to talk to China on the subject, and that China was the intransigent party. On 9 July 1998, India offered a bilateral No First Use Agreement to the Chinese. Were the Chinese to accept the offer, they would be seen as breaking ranks with the P-5, thus endangering the united front against India that China had worked so hard to steer in Geneva and New York. The Indian Government never seriously expected China to agree and, predictably, Beijing poured cold water on the whole proposal by insisting that India should first accede to the NPT and CTBT. But it served India's purpose of appearing flexible and conciliatory. China, on the other hand, was seen to be refusing to engage diplomatically at any level. Their Ambassador to Delhi, Zhou Gang, was a seasoned South Asia hand who belonged to the old school of Zhou Enlai diplomacy. He might have proved a good interlocutor, but the Chinese policy of 'coolness and isolation' made such efforts on his part difficult.

The Indian side continued to publicly demonstrate good intention. Jaswant Singh met Chinese Foreign Minister Tang Jiaxuan on the margins of the ASEAN Regional Forum meeting in Manila at the end of July 1998. He has written his account of this meeting in his autobiography.[34] He played on the Chinese concern with their self-image as a responsible global power that was not a threat to others. This was a Chinese weakness. It was at this meeting that Tang Jiaxuan had used the Chinese proverb 'he who ties the knot around the tiger's neck should also be the one to untie it' to define his expectations from India. The cat-and-mouse game with the Chinese continued throughout 1998. In October, National Security Advisor Brajesh Mishra made a pointed statement to the effect that India did not regard China as an enemy and had no intention of engaging in an arms race with it.[35]

Again, India showed to the rest of the international community that it was willing to address Chinese concerns and work with them. The Chinese remained unmoved and maintained their posture of no contact. Others, besides the Americans, also began talking to India. This included the British, the French and the Russians. China's policy led to its own self-isolation. An announcement on 7 November 1998 by the Clinton White House on the partial easing of sanctions on India and Pakistan, citing progress by India in declaring a moratorium on future testing and a public commitment to address US non-proliferation concerns, was a further blow to Chinese expectations that India would be punished by the international community until it yielded. Years later, Sha Zukang, who was regarded as China's point person on nuclear non-proliferation matters, would be bitter over the way in which the Americans and their allies had so quickly violated the common position taken by the P-5 in New York. He blamed the Americans for violating UN Security Council Resolution 1172 in pursuing nuclear cooperation with India. He felt that because of the bad example set by the US, its allies like France, Britain and Japan had followed suit.[36] In reality, the Chinese had themselves to blame. Sha Zukang and China had misread the Americans and misjudged India too.

By early 1999, the Chinese began to realize that the economic sanctions were not having the sort of devastating effect on the Indian economy that they had hoped for, and that it was, in fact, Pakistan that was the much more affected party. China also realized that the Americans had resiled from their earlier view that China could play some sort of a larger role in South Asia. Talbott's address to the Conference of Diplomacy and Preventive Defense at Palo Alto, California, on 16 January 1999, where he referred to China as 'an immensely complicating dimension'[37] in South Asia, was in marked contrast to the earlier US position that China was a positive factor for peace and stability in the region. Even in the sub-continent, events were transpiring to further dilute China's policy of 'coolness and isolation'. Vajpayee made his historic bus-ride to Lahore in February 1999 and, for a while, it appeared as if India and Pakistan might make a new beginning.

Why did China not anticipate these developments? While the Chinese had a solid system of academic research on a variety of foreign policy subjects supported by multiple think-tanks and research institutions, it is also true that the sort of speculative thinking that is permissible in other societies was not possible in China. In the case of India-related research, a set of relatively ageing academics, mostly on the wrong side of sixty, determined the 'line' on India. Since they were the only ones with access to policy-making circles, the younger researchers simply took their cue from the old guard. Despite the high degree of sophistication in research and the abundant resources that are now available to the Chinese think-tank community, it still continues to suffer from this problem, and perhaps this is even more the case in the New Era of Xi Jinping, because research is required to align to the Party line and not the other way around.

It was, finally, at some point at the turn of the new year (1999) that the Chinese finally realized that they were in a hole of their own making. They needed a way out from the impasse. The Indian leadership had correctly surmised that if they worked the international situation in their favour through the Americans while holding the line with China, the latter would eventually come around. Once it became evident that the Chinese were ready to re-engage with India, it was only a question of modalities, and here the Indian leadership was willing to offer the fig leaf for China to change tack. John Garver, in his essay in the *China Quarterly 2001*, has claimed that in late January 1999, India's President K.R. Narayanan did a '*mea culpa*' by acknowledging during a meeting with Chinese Ambassador Zhou Gang and former Ambassador Cheng Ruisheng in New Delhi that China did not constitute a threat to India. This was not accurate. In actual fact, the two Chinese diplomats had been invited to tea at Rashtrapati Bhavan (Presidential House) because the Chinese Embassy was offering to assist the President's spouse in publishing the Chinese edition of her book of short stories titled *Sweet and Sour* (this was later published and released during the President's visit to China in May–June 2000). However, in typical fashion, the Chinese used this meeting for their own purposes, and the Indian side did not make an issue of it, if it was going to serve to thaw the relationship.

Once the ice was broken, contact took place between the two foreign ministries. All previous attempts by the Indian Embassy in Beijing to propose various bilateral talks with the Chinese had

been met with studied silence. One of the difficulties in dealing
with the Chinese, even up to the present day, is the problem of
access. Unless they wish to meet you, it is virtually impossible to
meet them. In those days, mobile phones were rare and even the
internet was uncommon, and even today despite the advantages
of modern communications technology in the twenty-first century,
the problem remains. In early 1999, the Government of India
decided to probe the possibility of a dialogue with the Chinese
side, under the rubric of a protocol that had been signed between
the two foreign ministries which allowed for consultations to
take place from time to time. The Chinese agreed. This was
the first concrete indication to India that the Chinese may have
thought that the policy of 'coolness and isolation' had run its
course. Typically, the Chinese made it seem like it was India that
was looking to mend fences. The Joint Secretary for East Asia
(equivalent to Director General), therefore, travelled to China in
February 1999 for a meeting with his counterpart, the Director
General for Asian Affairs. This meeting consisted of accusations
and counteraccusations, and at one point devolved into a verbal
slanging match. This was intentional on the Chinese part. The
Chinese vented all their frustrations on the Indian delegation, but
they are also past masters in the art of perception management.
Hence, when the leader of the Indian delegation met with the
Assistant Foreign Minister Wang Yi (now the state councillor and
foreign minister of China) later that same afternoon, the latter
declared that the Sino-Indian relationship had returned to the
correct path. The meeting thus returned the two countries on the
path to normality. An immediate outcome was an invitation for
the External Affairs Minister to travel to Beijing.

Jaswant Singh visited China from 15 to 17 June 1999. By this
time, the Pakistani occupation of the heights above Kargil (on
the Line of Control in Jammu and Kashmir) had led to military
hostilities, and international public opinion had turned against

Pakistan. It had also proved embarrassing for China when a recording of the conversation between General Musharraf, who was in Beijing in the last week of May, and his Chief of Staff, General Aziz, was leaked in the media and established that Pakistan had been responsible for destabilizing the situation in South Asia. The visit of the Indian External Affairs Ministry delegation in February 1999 had helped open the blocked channels of communication to Chinese think-tanks and the Ministry of Foreign Affairs. The coordinated efforts of the Government of India in briefing the Chinese strategic community about the Kargil War, including on the basis of maps and other materials sent by Delhi, helped to build India's case with the Chinese that it was Pakistan that had provoked the tension. Thus, by the time Jaswant Singh arrived in Beijing in June 1999, the Chinese were finding it difficult to sustain their rhetoric or to isolate India. Typically, the Chinese tried to get Jaswant Singh to admit that it was all India's fault.

Foreign Minister Tang Jiaxuan trotted forth the Chinese proverb about untying the knot around the tiger's neck. Jaswant Singh's response was to quote a Rajasthani saying of his own— don't ask the way to a village if you don't intend to go there. In his own elegant way, and without publicly accepting that India had caused the trouble, Jaswant Singh provided good enough reason for the Chinese to tell the media that 'Sino-Indian relations have entered a process of improvement and Singh's visit to China is an important step in that process.'[38] With that statement, the knot came undone. Or, as the head of division looking after nuclear matters in the External Affairs Ministry* at the time and who was a member of the Indian delegation, put it, it 'brought closure' on the immediate matter at hand.[39]

The restoration of normal relations with China within a year of India's conducting the nuclear tests is an achievement of

---

* Rakesh Sood, joint secretary (Disarmament and International Security Affairs).

Indian foreign policy. This time, India had seized the initiative and held on to it; both by surprising China with nuclear tests which they had presumed were not an option that India had after the NPT Review Conference and the CTBT, and in strategically engaging the Americans while tactically engaging the Chinese. On the other hand, the Chinese objectives of punishing India and protecting its own image by damaging that of India, was largely reactive. It misjudged both the Indian resolve and the American response. In time, the China Threat theory would gain currency. Nor was China able to stop what it had feared, which is a growing convergence between India and the United States, which was to blossom under President George W. Bush. And, most importantly, it revived the issue of strategic 'parity' between India and China. Immediately after the tests, some Western academics opined that India could not achieve a core objective, that of dissuading the Chinese from supporting the Pakistan nuclear programme. This was never in fact an objective. India had hoped that the full normalization of relations following the visit of Prime Minister Rajiv Gandhi to China in December 1988 might lead the Chinese to re-consider their nuclear assistance to Pakistan, but this did not happen. Hence, the Indian side had no illusions about the nature of the Sino-Pak nuclear alliance by the time of India's nuclear tests. India would continue to raise this subject in order to keep reminding the Chinese about an inconvenient truth, namely that they were a factor in the global proliferation of nuclear weapons. This is a fact that the Chinese preferred the world forget.

What are the lessons to be drawn from the Chinese behaviour? One important lesson is the outsized importance that China attaches to its image. This is so because the Chinese State and the Communist Party of China are one and the same. The Chinese Communist Party derives its own legitimacy in part from the image it portrays to its people. While the authoritarian system is conducive to image-shaping within China, the international environment is more difficult for China to control because it is open and democratic. Hence, China expends substantial diplomatic capital in image-building abroad. This includes grand spectacles like the 2008 Beijing Olympic Games and the 2016 G-20 Summit in Hangzhou as well as projections of China as a benign and reasonable power globally as well as in the Indo–Pacific. This image is important for the Communist Party not so much internationally as domestically. It is a part of the image-cultivation that the Party does to earn legitimacy in the eyes of its own people. Much of the time the rest of the world buys into this image because of China's global importance, but this is also a vulnerability. The Chinese leadership is thin-skinned; unsettling them by impugning their self-image and how they want the rest of the world to view them can work to the other side's advantage.

Chinese behaviour during the episode of India's nuclear tests also uncovered another aspect of their diplomacy, this being that the Chinese will try to pursue their intended policy by hiding behind other countries or international public opinion. By claiming that China was only following the American lead and acting in line with international public anger against nuclear testing by India, it was initially able to disguise its own anti-India strategy and appear reasonable. As China has gained experience in multilateral diplomacy, it has begun to use this tool more effectively. It is now able to manipulate the system in order to stall and, if required, even to block outright, any developments that do not align with its core objectives, but always in the company of others. The trick lies in separating the Chinese from the pack, and in 'isolating' them, and thereafter keeping a steady course even if the Chinese use methods like intimidation, falsehoods, victimhood or fear psychosis to put maximum pressure on the perceived rival or adversary to change course.

If this does not succeed, China eventually reconciles to the situation and tries to find a way out. The Indian experience in 1998–1999 showed that a clear strategy coupled with a cogent and logical argument or narrative, and the ability to stay the course, could get the Chinese to change course. If the fog of confusion that China generates can be successfully dispelled and China's self-interest is exposed for all the world to see, the Chinese look for pragmatic solutions that will extricate them from the immediate quagmire in a way that allows them to claim victory in the eyes of the Chinese people.

IV

Sikkim: Half a Linguistic Pirouette

Tibet and Sikkim have a chequered history of tutelage and vassalage due to their shared Himalayan Buddhist heritage. The Tibetans always regarded Sikkim as theirs until the British Empire in India began its northward expansion in the nineteenth century. China, too, has claimed vassalage over Sikkim, Nepal and Bhutan during the Qing Empire (1644–1911). Two treaties between the Sikkim Raja and the British, in 1817 and in 1861, gave the British a degree of control over Sikkim, and more importantly, by the terms of the latter treaty, they also secured the right to trade with Tibet through Sikkim territory. Two routes through Sikkim, in particular, were viewed by the British as promising, Khamba Dzong and the Chumbi Valley.

In 1885, Coleman Macaulay, the Secretary to the Government of Bengal, decided to open trade relations with Tibet. The Tibetans did not share his enthusiasm and, having got wind of this intention, they invaded Sikkim territory from the Chumbi Valley through Jelep La (pass), and proceeded to occupy Lingtu which, according to the British, lay eighteen or so miles inside Sikkim. After failing to persuade the Tibetans to leave, a British expeditionary force under Brigadier General Thomas Graham advanced on Lingtu and expelled the Tibetans, although the Tibetans made further efforts to reclaim this area.[1]

When, therefore, in 1889, the Chinese Imperial Envoy (known as Amban) in Lhasa proposed an agreement with the British on the Tibet–Sikkim frontier, the British and Chinese empires negotiated and signed the Convention between Great Britain and China Relating to Sikkim and Tibet, in Calcutta (Kolkata) on 17 March 1890. By signing such a treaty, the Chinese Empire accepted that Sikkim belonged to the British sphere of influence. The Tibetans claimed that they were not part of these negotiations and neither did they acquiesce to this Convention, nor to the subsequent Trade Regulations signed on 5 December 1893, which opened the Chumbi Valley to trade for all British subjects from 1 May 1894. The Tibetans continued to view Sikkim as subordinate to Lhasa, and used every opportunity to demonstrate their control, including by reoccupying some places in north-east Sikkim that the 1890 Convention had placed within the Sikkim territory, and by demolishing border pillars that the British had tried to erect on the boundary. In 1895, after the Tibetans demolished a pillar at Jelep La, the Government of Bengal informed the Secretary of State for India in London that it was abandoning its efforts to demarcate the boundary. No further effort was made by the British Indian Government to demarcate the Tibet-Sikkim boundary on the ground.

In 1904, weary of Tibetan intransigence in accepting the boundary and trading arrangements negotiated between the British and the Chinese, the Government of India sent Sir Francis Younghusband with a military force into Lhasa. The resultant convention between Great Britain and Tibet (known as the Lhasa Convention of 7 September 1904), compelled the Dalai Lama's government to recognize the frontier between Sikkim and Tibet as defined by the 1890 Anglo–Chinese Convention. With the Chinese and Tibetans on the same page, so to speak, the British government could have resumed the process of demarcation of the Sikkim–Tibet boundary that was interrupted in 1895. They chose not to do so. The crumbling Chinese Empire, in a last gasp, launched a military campaign in Tibet under Chao Erh-feng, the Imperial Viceroy, and occupied Lhasa, thereby distracting the Tibetans from creating further problems on the Sikkim–Tibet frontier.[2] Soon thereafter in 1911, the Chinese Empire itself collapsed, and the British were left as the sole dominant power in the Himalayas. Hence the British might not, any longer, have considered the Sikkim–Tibet border to be an immediate problem for the British Indian Empire's Himalayan frontier. They never resumed the process of demarcation. This British decision would return to haunt India–China relations in the twenty-first century.

Following the independence of India in 1947, the new Government of India entered into a new treaty with Sikkim in 1950 under which it became a protectorate. Sikkim's defence, foreign affairs and communications were to be handled by the Government of India. Hence, when boundary negotiations began with China in the late 1950s, the Sikkim-Tibet frontier was deemed by the Indian side to be a part of the agenda for the India–China boundary talks. In 1956, Chinese Premier Zhou Enlai acknowledged the special relations that India had with Sikkim, but subsequently avoided any discussion with India on the Tibet–Sikkim boundary during the border talks in the late 1950s and in the official level talks in 1960. In fact, Premier Zhou wrote to Nehru on 8 September 1959 making it clear that the boundary between China and Sikkim 'does not fall within the scope of our present discussion . . .'[3]

This was no coincidence; it is now known that the Chinese were already aware of correspondence between the Government of India and the Dalai Lama's government in 1948 (before the founding of the People's Republic of China), wherein the Tibetan government had demanded that independent India should first return all the lands occupied by the British Empire. Sikkim was one of the territories claimed by them.[4] A cable from the Chinese Foreign Ministry to their ambassadors in July 1955, which contained several suggestions to strengthen ties with Afro-Asian nations, contained instructions to the effect that 'we should formulate a secret stipulation on the status of Sikkim, Bhutan, Kanjuti, etc.'[5] In 1954, the Chinese published a map showing Sikkim as a part of China.[6] These instances suggest that the new Communist government in Beijing wanted to keep all options open, including the Tibetan claims over Sikkim. Although they were in no position at that point of time to challenge India over Sikkim, Zhou Enlai shrewdly declined to engage in any activity that might suggest China's *de jure* recognition of Sikkim as a protectorate of India. For this reason, when India proposed that the boundary discussions should include the Sikkim–Tibet (China) sector, the Chinese Ministry of Foreign Affairs wrote to the Indian Embassy in Beijing on 26 December 1959, saying that 'the boundary between China and Sikkim has long been formally delimited and there is neither any discrepancy between the maps nor any disputes in practice.'[7] When Indian Ambassador Parathasarathi paid his farewell call on Vice Foreign Minister Geng Biao in Beijing on 19 July 1961, the Head of the Asian Department, Zhang Wenjin, who was also present, even alleged that India was wilfully trying to involve China in order to pressurize Sikkim (and Bhutan) into accepting India's version of where their boundaries with China lay.[8] In reality, the Chinese were buying time, and possibly studying records, while they made up their minds about Tibetan claims on Sikkim as well as the Anglo-Chinese discussions in earlier periods that had led to the 1890 and 1906 Conventions between Britain and China.

The Sikkim issue remained dormant after the 1962 border conflict, aside from the skirmishes between the Indian and Chinese forces along the Tibet-Sikkim boundary until 1973, when the Chinese grew concerned about India's attempts to change the status quo. The story of Sikkim's merger with India has been beautifully narrated by a number of those who were involved in the process, and it is not the subject of this book. Suffice to say that the process that commenced in May 1973 with the signing of the Tripartite Agreement, awoke the Chinese to a new situation developing on their Tibet frontier. A flurry of media attacks followed, labelling Indian activity in Sikkim as 'expansionist' and even drawing comparisons between the Soviet invasion of Czechoslovakia in 1968 in the name of protecting socialism and Indian action in Sikkim in the name of promoting democracy.[9] Some Chinese media pieces suggested that this was a Soviet plot to encircle China. The Chinese Communist Party mouthpiece, the *People's Daily*, called the merger 'a flagrant act of colonial expansion',[10] darkly warning India's other neighbours that what was being done by India to Sikkim would one day befall them as well. Chinese concerns over the changing status quo also figured in conversations with the Americans. In his talk with Secretary of State Dr Henry Kissinger in November 1974, Vice Premier Deng Xiaoping wondered aloud as to why India had wanted to annex Sikkim when they already had good control over it, and described Indian policy as 'something peculiar'.[11] Ambiguity over the status of Sikkim, which had served China well until 1974, was no longer tenable. On 11 September 1974, the Chinese Foreign Ministry issued a statement: 'The Chinese Government solemnly states that it absolutely does not recognize India's illegal annexation of Sikkim and that it supports the people of Sikkim in their just struggle for national independence and sovereignty and against Indian expansion.'[12] This position was reiterated on 29 April 1975, the day after Sikkim acceded to the Union of India. Thus, an issue that China had claimed was not a subject for discussion between India and China, now became a bone of contention between them.

The Chinese were conscious that they were the only country that refused to recognize the merger as legitimate. However,

China is never shy of standing alone on any matter that it deems to be of core interest, until it has weighed all the consequences. In an interview given by Deng Xiaoping to Krishna Kumar, the Editor of *Vikrant* magazine, in Beijing in June 1980, he said, 'We are opposed to the elimination of one sovereign state by another country. But we are not in a position to raise this question now.'[13] This sounded similar to Zhou Enlai's statement during the 1954 Tibet talks, that both sides should only take up issues ripe for settlement. Sikkim, therefore, became a card for the Chinese to be played to advantage when the opportunity presented itself, possibly even as a part of the so-called 'package deal' on the boundary question.

That chance was to come after India–China relations were normalized following the visit of Prime Minister Rajiv Gandhi in December 1988. The Government of India pressed hard upon the Chinese side to recognize the accession of Sikkim to India. In February 1990, when the minority government of Prime Minister Chandra Shekhar was in office, China's Foreign Minister Qian Qichen told External Affairs Minister Vidya Charan Shukla that China's public silence over Sikkim for several years in spite of its firm opposition to the 'illegal annexation' should be construed by India in a positive light.[14] From this point on, the Chinese position began to gradually unfold. Their strategy had three elements: strategically they would use the Sikkim Question as leverage for extracting concessions from India; optically they would appear as principled; tactically they would be flexible.

What were these Chinese objectives? First, the Chinese remained concerned about Tibet and the presence of the 14th Dalai Lama in India. Despite three decades of absolute control after the Dalai Lama had fled Tibet in March 1959, there was fresh unrest inside Tibet in 1989 (the thirtieth anniversary of the Dalai Lama's departure). Monks immolated themselves. The Chinese had to declare martial law in Lhasa in March 1989. The tenth Panchen

Lama's death in the same year was also another problem; the Tibetans refused to recognize the Chinese candidate. In December 1988, the Chinese had persuaded Prime Minister Rajiv Gandhi to acknowledge that Tibet was a part of the People's Republic of China, but he did so in a rather roundabout fashion and only as an 'autonomous region'. The Chinese believed they might use Sikkim for wresting a further admission of their sovereignty over Tibet from India. Second, Tibet's economic development had become a priority for the Chinese government in the 1990s, and trade with India offered an immediate opportunity for Tibet's development, as the road and rail links that have subsequently joined Tibet to the rest of China were absent at the time. Using Sikkim as the point of entry for Chinese products into India also circumvented the complications of doing trade across a disputed frontier. The Tibet–Sikkim boundary was the only part of the India–China boundary that China did not contest. As China's economy expanded, this option, thus, gained attraction. Not only did it, theoretically, allow for access to the Indian market but it was also an outlet for China to the Bay of Bengal and the Indian Ocean through the shortest possible route from the Chinese mainland. Thirdly, a settlement over Sikkim would also help to address China's image problem in India and show it to be a reasonable neighbour in South Asia, thus helping to overcome the trust deficit.

Chinese tactics were to engage in wordplay. Chinese Premier Li Peng told Prime Minister P.V. Narasimha Rao, during the latter's official visit to Beijing in September 1993, that China was willing to take a 'flexible attitude' on the Sikkim Question by proceeding on a more or less realistic basis, and taking into account the interests of the people of India and Sikkim.[15] This was a clever formulation, because by making a reference to the people of Sikkim as distinct from the people of India, it still allowed the Chinese to keep their position on the status of Sikkim open to all possibilities while offering India a glimmer of hope. They had succeeded with such double-speak on the status of Jammu and Kashmir with India in the 1950s, and it had become a part of their playbook. The Chinese signal flexibility through the clever use of optics in order to draw the other party into the process of negotiation, whereafter the second party feels obligated to reciprocate by being flexible on the substantive issue, or of otherwise appearing to be unreasonable. Had the Government of India risen to the Chinese bait by being 'flexible', India would have fallen into their trap.

When the Chinese realized that the Indian side was not rising to their bait of finessing the Sikkim Question in a very roundabout fashion, they decided to leverage India's hope for a more formal Chinese recognition of Sikkim as a part of India, in return for important trade and other concessions. Suggestions were made by the Chinese side, at all levels, at first obliquely and then more directly, about the quid pro quo that China expected, which was the opening of the trade route through Sikkim. China also suggested that the military forces of the two sides could agree on a Border Personnel Meeting point on the Sikkim-Tibet boundary, and the exchange of international mail at Natu La, which was a border pass on the Sikkim-Tibet frontier.

None of these ideas were new or original. Before the boundary conflict occurred in 1962, trade between Sikkim and the Chumbi Valley in Tibet had been a regular activity since the early 1900s; mail was being exchanged at Natu La; and the two armies had continued to maintain an informal liaison on the Tibet-Sikkim frontier all through the freeze in diplomatic relations after 1962. None of these had meant that China recognized Sikkim as a State of India. In 1996, Chinese Foreign Minister Qian Qichen offered the idea to Foreign Minister I.K. Gujral that the re-opening of trade would be tantamount to an acknowledgement of the status quo by China.[16] It was a persuasive argument, and might have even sounded reasonable were it not for India's experience over a similar matter in the 1950s. The 1954 Trade Agreement between

India and the Tibet Region of China had, similarly, identified six border passes in the Middle Sector through which trade and other intercourse could take place between the Tibet region of China and India. India had assumed that this was tantamount to a recognition of where our boundary lay. The Chinese first kept their counsel, then dissimulated when pressed and finally said that the boundary had not been a subject for discussion at the time, and that the six passes named in the 1954 agreement were only a specific modality for a specific purpose—namely trade. Now, forty years later, the Chinese were offering up the same formula for Sikkim.

The Chinese case was that the 'process' of recognition had to be gradual, tantalizingly suggesting that a trade arrangement might be the first step, and thus subtly mounting pressure on the Indian side to be flexible and to not insist that the Chinese side bring a solution once and for all. The Chinese duplicity in 1954 was, however, seared into the mind of every diplomat who had seriously studied China, and they recognized it for what it was, a diplomatic bear-trap. There were sceptics inside the Indian establishment who derided such thinking as archaic or even obstructive. They felt that a bilateral agreement on border trade constituted a Chinese acknowledgement of the ground reality in Sikkim, and were confident that, in time, it would lead the Chinese to de jure recognition on Sikkim as a State of India. The solution to the Sikkim Question, therefore, tested the mettle of the Government of India in its entirety. Had the officials in the External Affairs Ministry buckled under pressure, the Chinese might have achieved their objectives rather easily. Fortunately, the attempts of the Gujral government to resolve the issue stalled with the change in government.

When the National Democratic Alliance Government of Prime Minister Atal Bihari Vajpayee took office in March 1998, the Governments of India and China almost immediately had to grapple with the fallout of India's nuclear tests on the bilateral relationship. This was followed by the Kargil conflict. Hence, in the first three years of Vajpayee's tenure, no real opportunity to resolve the Sikkim Question arose. The first opportunity that India got to raise this matter, once the two sides had put away the nuclear issue and restored normality in their relations, was in January 2002, when Chinese Premier Zhu Rongji came visiting New Delhi. His was the first visit at the level of Head of State or Government from the Chinese side since President Jiang Zemin's visit in November 1996. India was fortunate that it had, in Prime Minister Vajpayee and his National Security Advisor Brajesh Mishra, two individuals who had an excellent understanding of India–China relations. They had already initiated the exercise for clarification of the Line of Actual Control in 2000, and decided that it was the time to push the envelope on Sikkim. Vajpayee, therefore, raised the matter with Premier Zhu Rongji in private, in an anteroom, after the official talks. Premier Zhu heard Vajpayee out. As Premier Zhu was ascending in the elevator to return to his hotel suite after the official dinner hosted by Prime Minister Vajpayee, he told his colleagues of his conversation with the latter. Vajpayee, he said, had told him that the time had come to resolve the Sikkim Question. When a member of his entourage inquired as to what he had replied, Zhu said that he had told Vajpayee that he would consider the matter, whereupon Vajpayee had pressed the request. Premier Zhu asked the accompanying officials to study the matter upon their return to Beijing. Knowledge of this conversation came to light because a young, and exceptionally alert, officer who was present in the elevator as a liaison officer to the Chinese delegation, and who spoke Chinese fluently, promptly reported it to his superiors.[17] It is in this manner that the Indian side learned that the matter would be looked at afresh in Beijing after the Chinese Premier's return. This had been the objective of Prime Minister Vajpayee and his government.

In the summer of 2002, External Affairs Minister Jaswant Singh travelled to China for his second visit. He had developed a good equation with his counterpart, Foreign Minister Tang Jiaxuan. In his book, Jaswant Singh recalled that during this visit he had tentatively raised the question of Chinese recognition of Sikkim as a part of India with Tang Jiaxuan, and that it 'eventually resulted in the assurance that during the next visit of the Chinese Premier such an announcement would be made.'[18] Jaswant Singh had actually got the sequence a little mixed up. Jaswant Singh's very first meeting in Beijing was with Vice Premier Qian Qichen, who was the Politburo member responsible for overseeing China's foreign relations.[19]

Qian had come straight to the point on Sikkim, and suggested that border trade might be resumed immediately through Yadong in Tibet (Chumbi Valley), which had been the customary trade mart for centuries. Hence, Qian's idea was to offer recognition of the status quo in Sikkim in this indirect manner in exchange for the direct resumption of border trade. It is possible that the Chinese felt, after Prime Minister Vajpayee had raised the matter with Premier Zhu Rongji, that India was anxious to make progress and might agree if China offered the 1954 'Tibet formula' again. Subsequently, in the Foreign Minister level talks, Tang Jiaxuan spoke of a 'process', and suggested that both sides establish a mechanism at the official level to work out the details.[20] The proposal for a mechanism was particularly troublesome, because this would enable the Chinese to extract the maximum concessions without conceding their core position. It would have been difficult for India to come out of formal negotiation without results. Walking out of a negotiation was not an option. It was a repeat of tactics that the Chinese had followed with India at the time of diplomatic recognition.

The professionals in the Ministry of External Affairs cautioned Jaswant Singh about the Chinese intentions. Jaswant Singh was impatient and, perhaps, felt that his advisors were being over-cautious. In his memoirs, he described this evocatively as 'the official advice of caution; one step at a time or perhaps half a linguistic pirouette.'[21] In reality it was anything but a dance step. The advice took into account the lessons learned from the experience of India–China negotiations over Tibet in 1954. It is also important to look at Chinese behaviour when it concerned China's own sovereignty and territorial integrity. The People's Republic of China had not exercised sovereignty over the island of Taiwan for a single minute of a single day since they had founded the new government in Peking on 1 October 1949. Yet all foreign governments desiring to have a relationship with Beijing had to first explicitly recognize China's absolute and unconditional sovereignty over Taiwan.

No compromise was made by the Chinese on this principle, not with India in 1950 and not even with the United States of America in 1979, which was the most powerful nation at the time and the superpower with whom the Chinese desperately wanted to normalize relations. Sovereignty was a matter of principle for the Chinese that could not be sacrificed at any cost. On the other hand, the very same Chinese were proposing that India agree to China recognizing India's sovereignty and territorial integrity in an indirect way via a border trade agreement! That too with regard to a state over which India had exercised total sovereignty since 1975. This was not a question of tilting at windmills like some Don Quixote; it involved the principle of sovereignty. It was therefore important, and necessary, to insist that China should follow their own principle by explicitly recognizing Indian sovereignty over Sikkim before the opening of border trade and other exchanges.

Following the visit of External Affairs Minister Jaswant Singh to China, and as agreed by both sides, a mechanism was set up to begin negotiations on the text of a border trade agreement. In any negotiation, the written word matters, more so for the Chinese who have a long tradition of recording history unlike the *shruti* or oral tradition in India. The Chinese are skilful at manipulating words and their meanings; the possibility of a word or phrase having more than one meaning or being ambiguous, needs to be carefully parsed in a negotiation with the Chinese. The text of the border trade agreement suggested by the Chinese side contained the phrase 'border pass'. Prima facie this met Indian concerns. Except that the words 'border pass', unless it was qualified by reference to a particular geography, need not necessarily refer only to its location being on the India–China border; it was also open to being interpreted as the China–Sikkim border, since China had not explicitly recognized Sikkim as a part of India. Presuming Chinese silence to be tantamount to acquiescence, if not acceptance, had cost India dearly in the 1950s.

The Indian side, therefore, pressed upon the Chinese side to include an explicit geographical reference to confirm that the passes through which the border trade would be conducted were located on the India–China border. The Indian side also pressed for a clear iteration from China to describing the proposed trade marts on either side, at Changgu and Renqinggang, as 'Changgu, Sikkim, India' and 'Renqinggang, Tibet Autonomous Region, People's Republic of China'.[22] This might appear as semantics, but this was not a mistake to be made when negotiating with the Chinese. The Chinese officials resisted all efforts to add the country names. This strengthened the feeling on the Indian side that the Chinese were mendacious. However, Prime Minister Vajpayee was preparing to leave for his first official visit to China. The Chinese recognized that political pressure was mounting on Indian officials to conclude an agreed text before Vajpayee's first visit to China as Prime Minister in June 2003. China was hoping that this pressure would force India to compromise on its 'all-or-nothing' approach.

The Chinese pressure tactic worked. The Chinese strung the Indian side along until the border trade agreement was nearly ready and the visit of the Indian Prime Minister was imminent, before they reverted to their old talk of recognition of Sikkim being a 'gradual process'. At this point, the political dispensation in India might have felt the need for a major foreign policy achievement before the 2004 general election. The desire to sound the trumpets seemed to be so strong that the Government of India might not have been able to resist the temptation to sign the trade agreement and claim that they had got the Chinese to recognize Sikkim as part of India, without getting an explicit political pronouncement to that effect by China. Had the Indian side insisted until the very end about securing a political iteration from China that Sikkim was part of India, the Chinese may have relented eventually since they also wanted an iteration of their own from India, on Tibet. They wanted a formulation that improved upon what Prime Minister Rajiv Gandhi had given them in 1988, namely that Tibet was an autonomous region of the People's Republic of China, with a much more explicit acknowledgement. In the end, the Chinese did not explicitly acknowledge in the Joint Statement issued at the end of the Vajpayee visit that Sikkim was a part of India, but India on its part added further legitimacy to the Chinese claim over Tibet by averring in the Joint Statement that 'Tibet Autonomous Region is part of the territory of the People's Republic of China'. By itself, this statement by India was not problematic because India already considered Tibet in this way since 1954. But a unilateral declaration by India in a bilateral Joint Statement on a matter concerning the sovereignty and integrity of China on the matter of Tibet, without India securing a corresponding political recognition from China that Sikkim was part of the territory of the Republic of India, seemed like poor execution. India got half a victory when she might have had it all.

It fell to the next Government, led by Prime Minister Dr Manmohan Singh, to complete the process by securing, in the Joint Statement of 11 April 2005, the words 'Sikkim State of India'.[23] The Chinese agreed to this formulation because they wanted the Agreement on Political Parameters and Guiding Principles for the Settlement of the India–China Boundary Question, which was to be the centrepiece of the 2005 visit of Chinese Premier Wen Jiabao. The price that the Government of India had to pay was not just to reiterate the new formulation on Tibet—that it was a part of the PRC—that had been agreed upon by the predecessor government, but also to agree to elevate the relationship into a Strategic and Cooperative Partnership for Peace and Prosperity. It is another matter that few questioned how the two neighbours with an unresolved boundary of over 3000 kilometres, and with one partner unwilling to recognize the other's sovereignty and territorial integrity over large tracts of territory, could become strategic partners. It was only some years later that China finally changed its official maps to show Sikkim as a part of India.

China's recognition of Sikkim in 2005 represents an important milestone in India's China diplomacy. It demonstrates that the lessons of the 1950s had been heeded and internalized within the Government of India. On the Sikkim Question, India had resolved the question of sovereignty in a bold manner in the early 1970s when the situation in South Asia was in favour of India, Pakistan was divided and China was internally distracted by the Great Proletarian Cultural Revolution. All that remained after mid-1975 was for China to accept the new reality and with this clear objective in sight, India pursued it for over two decades with the Chinese side, without displaying either haste or anxiety and unmindful of failure. It offers a case study of how results are achieved when systems work.

The institutional memory within the government—because a trained cadre of officers on both the civilian and military sides that had worked on China, was available to offer insight and advice—guided the political leadership into side-stepping a number of traps that the Chinese had laid with the purpose of prolonging Chinese ambiguity on India's sovereign claims over Sikkim state, possibly in perpetuity. At the end, the compulsions of democracy might have led to India compromising on the ideal outcome. This is a pitfall that India shall have to deal with in the future as well, and one that the Chinese are beginning to exploit.

There are also lessons to be learned about the way that China negotiates. The Sikkim Question is a good example of how China sees others' problems as an opportunity to extract concessions or as leverage. Part of the tactic is deliberate ambiguity of position. The Chinese have developed this into a fine diplomatic tradition. The coming generations need to pay attention to what China does not say or do. The presumption that silence is acquiescence could be fatal for nations. A second takeaway is the Chinese practice of testing the Indian bottom line multiple times. China can repeat a position ad nauseam, until the other party, in sheer frustration, puts a revised offer on the table. The repetition of position at multiple meetings fulfils two objectives—it allows the Chinese to understand the time-table of the other side in resolving an issue, and it allows them to test the other side's bottom line. Both are leveraged for benefit. In the case of the Sikkim Question, the Indian bottom line remained unshakeable, but the time-table offered up the opportunity for China to secure other political objectives. It is not a pleasant situation when lack of progress leads to temporary setbacks, but this should be accepted as a part of doing diplomacy with China.

The saga of Sikkim is still not over. As China continues to progress towards becoming the world's largest economy and trading nation, the need for secure outlets to the oceans will grow. Sikkim's importance to China is growing by the day. If China can persuade India in the future to permit Chinese merchandise to transit Sikkim, it will be a 'golden goose'. It will allow China to transport goods in a secure and commercially profitably way overland through Tibet to the Indian heartland, where half a billion Indians live, thus giving it access to a major global market that is not dependent on transit through any other country. It will, equally importantly, become the shortest route from mainland China to the Bay of Bengal and the Indian Ocean. The port of Kolkata is just 725 kilometres away from the Tibet frontier in Sikkim. In contrast, the China–Pakistan corridor is over 1500 kilometres and the China–Myanmar corridor is over 1100 kilometres, and both cross inhospitable terrain and politically unstable territories. The transit through Sikkim is, therefore, the most viable route for China to the Indian Ocean, and Sikkim becomes a good bet for China to overcome their Malacca Dilemma. The Chinese will, therefore, continue to make strenuous efforts to persuade India to open this route. Their offer to settle the India–China boundary in the Sikkim Sector as an 'early harvest' is basically linked to this objective.

If India accepts the idea, it will be akin to Adam accepting the proverbial forbidden fruit in the Garden of Eden. The consequences could be potentially devastating. In a single diplomatic gambit, the Chinese will secure three prized objectives—direct overland access to the huge Indian domestic market; the shortest route to the Bay of Bengal and the Indian Ocean; and never having to finalize the India–China boundary in any other sector since they can trade freely with India without finalizing a disputed frontier.

In a nutshell, giving them access through Sikkim (or for that matter through Nepal) might mean that China will have no compelling reason to seek a boundary settlement until a time of their choosing. Moreover, the opening of regular overland trade between India and China through Khamba Dzong and the Chumbi Valley will also, unquestionably, set off a chain of events that might compel the Royal Government of Bhutan to open its frontiers to the Chinese, and generate pressure from the Government of Bangladesh to allow transit through the Siliguri Corridor for trade with China. It will constitute the final breach in the Himalayan barrier that Deputy Prime Minister Vallabhbhai Patel had spoken about in his letter to Prime Minister Jawaharlal Nehru on 7 November 1950. For that reason, a settlement of the India–China boundary in the Sikkim Sector should only be a part of the final and comprehensive settlement.

V

123 Deal: The Big Turnabout

Following India's Peaceful Nuclear Explosion (PNE) in May 1974, the United States initiated a move to punish India by creating a multilateral export control regime on the pretext that nuclear technology transfers for peaceful purposes could be misused by non-nuclear weapon states for their nuclear weapons programmes.[1] It was called the Nuclear Suppliers Group (NSG). Two sets of guidelines were established for nuclear exports and nuclear-related exports, and the membership was systematically expanded to rope in any Nuclear Non-Proliferation Treaty (NPT) signatory who had the relevant technologies. Although it was never stated that India was the target, an important intent was to cripple India's nuclear weapons research and development. China was not a founder-member of the NSG. In fact, in 1975, China was not a signatory to the NPT either.

India's decision to test in May 1998 was influenced by many factors and is not the subject of this book. The tests demonstrated that while the US-led nuclear sanctions may have impacted India's nuclear weapon capabilities, it had been unsuccessful in putting a complete stop to it. The mutual desire of India and America to reset their relations post-Pokhran, which gained in momentum under the Presidency of George W. Bush, provided India with a fresh opportunity to break out of the nuclear sanctions. The NSG guidelines had crippled India's nuclear energy programme, and with the looming climate change crisis threatening to 'outlaw' coal, the need for clean energy gained priority.

The opportunity presented itself when Prime Minister Dr Manmohan Singh made an official visit to Washington in July 2005 and, with President Bush, announced their intention to enter into a nuclear energy agreement. The following March (2006), during President Bush's return visit, the two sides reached an agreement on a separation plan that made bilateral civil nuclear cooperation, and nuclear trade for India with the rest of the world, a real possibility for the first time in three decades.

After the end of the Cold War, other important changes were also taking place in the global nuclear landscape. America had led a global initiative to destroy nuclear weapons in the possession of successor states of the Soviet Union (other than the Russian Federation); more nuclear weapon states had emerged—Pakistan and North Korea; while still others, like Iraq, Libya and Iran, were suspected of having active nuclear weapons programmes. Non-proliferation was a raison d'être for the Americans to invade Iraq. And China had come out of the nuclear cold, finally joining the NPT in 1992 and the NSG in 2005. The NSG membership had expanded to 47 countries (from the initial seven). The expanded membership of the NSG was a sign of growing international concerns over the possible proliferation of nuclear weapons and technology. In this context, the Indo–US nuclear deal was seen in some quarters as a free pass for India, without corresponding commitments to the NPT regime. Nonetheless, America was the world's only super-power, and the NSG's endorsement of the India–US nuclear deal in terms of giving India a clean waiver to source nuclear technology and materials without signing the NPT, while likely to face many problems including from friendly

European states and non-aligned countries, was still an objective worth pursing. France* and the United Kingdom were expected to follow the American lead; Russia was favourable. China, however, was a question mark.

The upheaval that the Indian nuclear tests in 1998 had caused in India–China relations had been smoothed over by 2003, but within China it had led to a re-evaluation of India generally and, more specifically, of India's nuclear programme. The simplistic explanation for this re-evaluation was that China now had an overt nuclear weapons state on its disputed south-western border that had also levelled allegations about China being a threat in order to justify India's nuclear tests. However, the fact remains that the tests did not significantly change the ground realities for China; what did change was the perception that China was no longer the sole Asian nuclear weapons state. After India had tested in 1998, China's approach on the Nuclear Question vis-à-vis India was shaped by two concerns. One was over the convergences between the Americans and India, and the conclusion of the Indo–US nuclear deal suggested to the Chinese that such convergences were growing. Another concern arose from the challenge that the Indian nuclear tests posed to the carefully constructed Chinese narrative that China was the sole legitimate Asian nuclear weapons state.

In the early 1960s, the Chinese had already guessed that India was also developing nuclear weapons technology. Yet their carefully constructed narrative did not make mention of India's capabilities, but instead focused on the ten-year gap in the testing cycle (China tested in 1964 and India in 1974), in order to justify their contention that in 1968, when the NPT was adopted, India did not have the capacity to test a nuclear weapon and, hence, could not be a nuclear weapons state under the NPT. This is the perception they wished to create even though the reality

---

* French support predated the 18 July agreement.

was different. Declassified papers show that India's chief atomic scientist, Homi J. Bhabha, had written letters to Prime Minister Nehru in 1963 about India possessing the capability to test a nuclear weapon.[2]

The Americans were independently aware of India's capabilities in that regard. A telegram from the US State Department in March 1966 referred to the probability that India would be in a position to test a nuclear device within a year of such a political decision being made by the Indian leadership.[3] The reason for India not testing before the NPT was signed in 1968 was not, perhaps, because India did not possess the technology; it lay elsewhere. India was seeking iron-clad guarantees from the Americans and the Soviets that they would individually or together come to India's assistance in the event of a Chinese attack. Prime Ministers Lal Bahadur Shastri and Indira Gandhi actively explored this possibility with the Johnson administration.

There were conversations in Delhi between US Special Envoy Averell Harriman and Shastri in 1965,[4] and between the Indian Prime Minister's Secretary L.K. Jha and President Johnson in 1967.[5] America refused to give specific guarantees, mainly out of concern that exclusive nuclear guarantees to India would alienate Pakistan, which was a strategic ally. A memo in this regard from General Curtis LeMay, Acting Chairman, Joint Chiefs of Staff, to Robert McNamara, Secretary of Defence, became the foundation of US nuclear policy towards India.[6] In short, India not testing a nuclear device before 1968 may have had less to do with technical capability and more to do with the lack of political will. The evidence suggests, therefore, that China's narrative about India lacking the capability to explode a nuclear device before the NPT was signed, is both specious and self-serving. The question is why did China construct this narrative?

From the very beginning, China had a clear vision about nuclear weapons. China's first-generation leadership led by Mao Zedong saw nuclear weapons as a counter-power to American bullying, and they built the bomb. Its second-generation leadership led by Deng Xiaoping leveraged the bomb as a means to demonstrate that China was a responsible member of the international community, by steering China first into the International Atomic Energy Agency in 1984 and then into the NPT in 1992. The subsequent generations of leaders, in the post-Cold War period, saw nuclear weapons as a guarantor of China's status as a true world power with no equal other than the United States, especially in the Indo–Pacific region. To maintain this image, it was essential for China to preserve strategic asymmetry both in terms of optics and in terms of ground realities with other aspirants, especially India which had tested a device in 1974. Until 1998, China could project the image of strategic asymmetry through two means: by claiming to be the only nuclear power in Asia because India and Pakistan had not yet declared themselves as nuclear weapons possessing states, and by manipulating the CTBT negotiations to try and lock India into permanent nuclear asymmetry with China. India's tests blew this policy out of the water. China, therefore, needed to construct a new narrative for preserving its strategic asymmetry in the twenty-first century.

China's objective even after the Indian nuclear tests in 1998 remained consistent—the preservation of strategic asymmetry vis-à-vis India and sustaining the perception that China was the only legitimate nuclear weapons state in Asia. The Chinese academic and strategic community set about assessing the implications of India's nuclear tests for China in order to build this new narrative. However, there was relatively little up-to-date research on India in the 1990s and early 2000s. A study conducted by a Chinese scholar and published by the Carnegie Endowment for International Peace in 2016, based entirely on Chinese sources about this subject, attests to the paucity of good information on India in general, and

India's strategic weapons programme in particular, in the public domain in China.[7] In the absence of original research, Chinese scholars still depended on Western literature.

The handful of Chinese literature that emerged on the Indian Nuclear Question in the early 2000s suggested that India had developed nuclear weapons because it wanted to be a Great Power; and also that she was using the 'China Threat' only to overcome substantial domestic and international opposition to her nuclear programme. The think-tank community remained convinced that despite the diplomatic recovery that India had made after 1998, the United States would never agree to relaxation in the nuclear sanctions imposed by the NSG and, consequently, India's existence outside the NPT regime would continue to marginalize it in international affairs. China could not visualize the possibility of sufficient convergences between India and America that might transcend the American concerns over non-proliferation in order to bring India into the nuclear fold. There was partial truth in all these Chinese assessments, but it did not take into account the changes in India–US relations since President Clinton's visit to India in 2000, as well as the changed internal political dynamics in India since the advent of the first NDA government. Thus, China's policy on the issue of the civil nuclear agreement and its strategy and subsequent negotiating position in the NSG, was flawed and proved to be ultimately unsuccessful.

Based on the assessment that there would be opposition both internally as well as in the West on any nuclear deal between India and the United States, a new three-pronged Chinese narrative unfolded after it became apparent that India and the US were seriously exploring a nuclear deal. The first message was for India, namely that China's nuclear posture was oriented towards the United States and, therefore, India had nothing to worry about. The second message was for the United States, namely that India's nuclear programme was oriented towards Pakistan (not China) over the Kashmir issue, and that South Asia was a powder keg prepped to explode into nuclear war. Thus, any latitude given to India in the NSG should be looked at not simply in terms of India's energy needs but in the context of possible nuclear conflict in South Asia. The third message was for the rest of the international community, namely, that they had helped to build the non-proliferation regime brick-by-brick through sacrifices, and any weakening of the multilateral regime would increase the dangers of nuclear conflict for all. Therefore, India's case should be viewed as the thin end of the wedge that could lead to the collapse of the whole structure with consequent danger to the world.

Having divided the strategy into three distinct parts, China proceeded to diplomatically deal with each of them.

Tackling India was complicated. On the one hand, China was distrustful of India. On the other hand, the restoration of ties after the 1998 nuclear tests had brought tangible benefits for China, including in the form of progress on the settlement of the Boundary Question (The Agreement on Political Parameters and Guiding Principles for Settlement of the India–China Boundary Question) and clear iteration by both major political parties, the BJP and the Congress, of Tibet being an integral part of the People's Republic of China. China decided to take a 'soft' public approach in India. Tactically, therefore, in their public pronouncements, the Chinese engaged in soft double-speak. The official position articulated by their spokespersons said: 'The Chinese side believes all countries can launch cooperation for peaceful uses of nuclear energy while abiding by respective international obligations. At the same time, such cooperation should be conducive to upholding and strengthening the principles and effectiveness of the principle of international nuclear non-proliferation.'[8]

Such pronouncements left enough room for optimism in India about China's reasonableness, and also preserved China's

positive image in Indian public opinion, which was expecting
China to openly oppose India's application to the NSG. Few
Indians read between the lines or cared to understand that the
thrust of the Chinese position was that India's adherence to
the NPT should be a pre-condition for any relaxation in NSG
guidelines for India. This soft public approach was combined
with evasive replies whenever Indian representatives raised the
NSG issue with Chinese counterparts. This issue was raised
on more than one occasion by both the then External Affairs
Minister Pranab Mukherjee and National Security Advisor M.K.
Narayanan.[9] The Chinese would invariably respond by showing
'understanding' for India's position but always with the caveat
that all nuclear-related activity should be within the framework
of international obligations. Chinese counterparts never referred
directly to the NPT or the CTBT in these conversations. This is
a typical Chinese negotiating tactic that is designed to generate
hope in the opposite interlocutor that the door for further
discussion remains open, without disclosing the specific Chinese
position.

It is also ambiguous enough for China to go either way,
depending on how the matter unfolds. In the meantime, China
utilized the close connections with the Left parties in India. Top
leaders of the Communist Party of India and Communist Party
of India (Marxist) would travel to China for meetings or medical
treatment.[10] Both parties were avowedly nationalist when it came
to the Boundary Question and other matters of bilateral interest,
but the Chinese were aware that they had fundamental concerns
about the Indo–US nuclear deal.[11] Knowing the influence
that the Left parties wielded in the United Progressive Alliance
government of Dr Manmohan Singh, China perhaps played on
their fears about India's tilt to the Americans. This may have been
the first example of China's foray into domestic politics, but they
were careful to remain behind the scenes.

The second dimension of the Chinese strategy was tackling the Americans. Unlike in 1998, this time round, the Americans and the Chinese began on opposite sides. China had felt let down by the Americans in the aftermath of the 1998 Indian nuclear tests, and the feeling had grown that the US was looking at India as a regional counterbalance to China. The Indo–US nuclear deal was seen as further confirmation that these larger geo-strategic considerations were in fact in play. Initially, the Chinese took a studied position of silence vis-à-vis the Bush administration. They felt that the US non-proliferation community, which was still smarting over the fact of India's nuclear tests, would be able to stall any Indo–US deal. The Chinese would, therefore, draw attention to positions taken by the American non-proliferation lobby in order to urge the Bush administration to reconsider the matter.

The mainstream Chinese strategic community also believed that India's wish for strategic autonomy would act as an automatic check on the extent of Indo–US collaboration. Prominent Chinese writings of that period opined that India's goal was in fact to become an independent pole, and India would, therefore, be unwilling to accept any binding conditions for nuclear energy cooperation.[12] Even until the day before President Bush's arrival in India in March 2006, the Chinese had hoped that the Indo–US deal would fall through the large gap between the positions of India and the US. On the eve of Bush's visit, the *China Defence News* confidently wrote that the intention of the United States was to penetrate India's nuclear weapons programme in order to control it, and that the Indians would not allow this to happen.[13] Therefore, the nuclear deal would not be successfully concluded.

When, therefore, on 3 March 2006, President Bush and Prime Minister Singh signed a Joint Statement consummating nuclear cooperation, the Chinese were likely taken by surprise. While remaining poker-faced with India, the Chinese began to complain to the Bush administration on the issue. They voiced

their concerns that such a deal might help India's nuclear
weapons programme, and might even weaken India's pledge of
minimum credible deterrence. They also aligned with the US
non-proliferation community in supporting its efforts to lobby
Congress and the media. Internally, by this time, the Chinese
strategic community was veering around to the belief that the
US was trying to pull India into a strategic alliance and wanting
to monopolize the potentially large Indian market for nuclear
energy. Yet, even at this point, the Chinese still hoped that the
differences between India and America over the Separation Plan
and the issue of re-processing of spent fuel were so deep as to
be unbridgeable.[14] The Separation Plan was offered by India
to the International Atomic Energy Agency (IAEA), vide which
the Government of India undertook the following commitments:
identification and separation of civilian and military nuclear
facilities and programmes in a phased manner; filing a declaration
regarding its civilian facilities with IAEA; taking a decision to place
voluntarily its civilian nuclear facilities under IAEA safeguards;
and signing and adhering to an Additional Protocol with respect
to civilian nuclear facilities.

At least publicly, the Chinese stuck to their belief that India's
fear of alignment with the US and its wish to be an independent
great power, as well as the strong opposition inside India against a
closer alignment with the United States, would hold India back from
'band-wagoning' with the US.[15] It was only when the 'Agreement
for Cooperation Between the Government of the United States of
America and the Government of India concerning the Peaceful
Uses of Nuclear Energy' (known as the 123 Agreement) became
public in August 2007 that China's anxiety reached a level that
compelled an escalation in their tactics. It is also believed that it
was around this time that China decided to accelerate its nuclear
cooperation with Pakistan by 'grandfathering' a deal for new
nuclear reactors and also in other matters.

It was after the 123 agreement was concluded and India went to the IAEA while the Americans decided to move the NSG for a clean waiver, that China, having exhausted other tactics, made their unhappiness palpable to the Americans and decided to ratchet up their efforts to disrupt the process in the NSG by several notches. They trained their sights on the membership of the NSG. The Chinese were well aware that within the international community, the general concerns over nuclear proliferation were growing due to the pursuit of nuclear weapons by Kim Jong Il of North Korea, Muammar Gaddafi of Libya and by the religious leadership in Iran. The US-led global nuclear crusade had created an entire community of experts and officials who lived and breathed non-proliferation.

Although the Soviet threat had substantially reduced for Europe in 1991, the characterization of several states as the 'Axis of Evil' by the Bush presidency had dovetailed with the War on Terror to create the ultimate spectre of nuclear terrorism, especially for the smaller Western states. China decided to play on their concerns. It helped that China was by now within the NSG (this was not the case in 1998). Chinese diplomats began to work on the NSG members, especially the 'purists', highlighting that, on the one hand, the Americans had called for the strengthening of the international non-proliferation regime to deprive the 'rogue' states of their right to have nuclear energy while, on the other hand, it was violating the existing international rules and regulations to help India when it suited the global interests of America. Well-respected Chinese commentators such as the former Chinese Ambassador to India Cheng Ruisheng wrote about the 'big turn-about' that America had made.

'The fact that the United States could give up part of its interests on non-proliferation in order to realize its strategic objective of forming an alliance with India has fully reflected the flexibility of US policy,' he wrote.[16] The *World Affairs* magazine, which was published under the aegis of the Chinese Foreign Ministry, posited that India was dangling civil nuclear cooperation as a bait to break down the restrictions imposed by the NSG and to get parity with the nuclear weapons states.[17] Such arguments were intended to scare the small Western countries and to strengthen the resolve of the opposition, especially the so-called Group of Six—Ireland, New Zealand, Austria, Switzerland, Norway and the Netherlands. This was classic Chinese diplomacy, what former NSA S. Menon called a form of diplomatic guerrilla warfare.[18] China hid behind the curtain and manipulated the 'purists' in the NSG, much like Ci Xi, Dowager Empress of China had done with Emperor Guang Xu at the end of the nineteenth century.

India had learned from the experience of dealing with China in 1998–1999. This time, unlike at the time of the nuclear tests, the Chinese were briefed early in New Delhi along with the other Permanent Members and some important countries. The text of the 123 Agreement was shared with them. India offered to send a political-level Special Envoy to China.[19] The possibility of collaborating with China in civil nuclear energy after the NSG waiver was also held out. Prime Minister Dr Manmohan Singh personally raised the matter with both Premier Wen Jiabao in Singapore in November 2007 and with President Hu Jintao in Beijing in January 2008. China could not claim, this time, that India had gone behind her back or painted her as a villain. When India's National Security Advisor M.K. Narayanan met Premier Wen Jiabao in Beijing in late September 2007, the Chinese were careful to underscore that it was China's strategic policy to improve ties with India, but did not raise the subject of the Indo–US nuclear deal.[20] In October 2007, at the Russia–India–China Foreign Ministers meeting, when this subject was indirectly brought up by External Affairs Minister Pranab Mukherjee in the context of access to affordable clean energy technology to meet India's commitments to climate change, Chinese Foreign Minister Yang

Jiechi briefly alluded to China's wish to see India join the CTBT, but again skirted around the issue of the nuclear deal.[21] In New Delhi, the Chinese Ambassador used to talk about China's efforts to work for a consensus with the other NSG members on India's case. It sounded positive, but it soon became apparent that the word 'consensus', in China's negotiating lexicon, was tantamount to a Veto of One. There was a desire on both sides to maintain a publicly amicable relationship, while each was engaged behind the scenes in pursuing their strategy.

India reached out to the other NSG members in Vienna and their capitals, and learned of Chinese efforts behind-the-scenes to block the NSG waiver. Reasonable doubts were raised by many countries, including those like Japan which wished to be helpful. These included concerns about proliferation by Pakistan in the event of a breach in the wall of nuclear non-proliferation, the question of safeguards, a more binding commitment from India on further nuclear testing, and on enrichment and reprocessing. In Vienna, New Delhi and in capitals of NSG countries, India worked to narrow the differences between the two 'camps' in the NSG. The Americans were working in tandem on their allies to convince the fence-sitters such as Mexico, Turkey and Egypt. By the time the NSG met in early August 2008 in Vienna, a number of countries had been persuaded to support the clean waiver for India, but significant opposition still remained. India made a last effort to reach out to the 'opposition'. The Minister of State in the Prime Minister's Office was sent to Beijing. Coincidentally, Sonia Gandhi, Chairperson of the United Progressive Alliance, was scheduled to travel for the Beijing Olympics at the same time that the matter came before the NSG.

On 1 August 2008, the board of governors of the IAEA unanimously approved the 'Agreement between Government of India and the IAEA for Application of Safeguards to Civilian Facilities', clearing the way for the matter to be taken up by the NSG.

China recognized that the matter was coming to a head but still hesitated to show its opposition openly. Their Ambassador to the IAEA referred to 'a number of countries' which had doubts or concerns about giving India a clear waiver, and hoped that all voices would be heard.[22] It also stuck to its ambiguous position of referring to the right to peaceful uses of nuclear energy in consonance with international non-proliferation obligations. When the NSG met in Vienna in early August 2008, discussion began on the US draft exemption. The US disarmed some critics of the deal by clarifying at the outset that it would not recognize India as a nuclear weapons state. Several smaller Western European states and New Zealand wanted new conditions to be written into the waiver, such as cessation of all assistance if India tested again. Large countries like Brazil and Russia sat on the sidelines. Japan remained silent although it had assured India that it would not oppose a consensus. China went public by asking that there should not be a single exception, but a criterion or rules-based decision applicable to all non-NPT signatories.

They deemed this to be a principle, which is another classic Chinese diplomatic ruse. This was a calculated Chinese attempt to include Pakistan in the exception. On 21–22 August 2008, the Group of Six tabled a series of 'killer' amendments to the American text, including a provision to terminate nuclear trade with India if it carried out further nuclear tests, that the waiver given to India should exclude Enrichment and Reprocessing Technologies, and a demand for a periodic review of India's compliance. These were designed to make the waiver 'conditional'. China lent quiet support. It also put up its own minor amendments with the intention of delaying the process. These amendments were contrary to India's wish for a clean waiver. Eventually, talks in Vienna in August 2008 ended in a deadlock. China assumed that the wall of opposition to making an exception for India was unbreachable.

This confidence was reflected, perhaps for the first time, in the Chinese official mouthpiece, the *People's Daily*, on 2 September 2008. It confidently declared that 'The Safeguards Agreement between the IAEA and India is a very loose non-binding agreement. It is neither clarified what kind of nuclear facilities should fall under IAEA supervision, nor stipulates if all civil nuclear facilities and fuel should be under permanent IAEA supervision. This has aroused concerns—is India enjoying the same rights as NPT Members without corresponding obligations?'[23] Here lay the heart of the Chinese argument, and thinking that there was sizeable opposition within the NSG, the Chinese felt confident enough to join the chorus, publicly.

They reckoned without the American resolve. The nuclear deal had become one of the defining legacies of the Bush administration, and it was determined to remove barriers to its successful conclusion. America was the world's only super-power; it was at its zenith. When the NSG resumed its meeting in early September 2008, China's official spokesman continued to say that there were different opinions in the NSG[24] and continued to hide behind them. However, in the recess, the American Secretary of State had worked the phones, speaking to Western counterparts, to drop their opposition.[25] The Group of Six, behind which China had hidden for so long, were picked off one-by-one, until on the night of 5 September, China remained the last man standing. They threatened to withdraw from the negotiations, which would have meant there was no consensus. It is reported that calls were made from Washington to Beijing at the highest levels in the administration. Simultaneously, at 3 a.m. in the early hours of 6 September, the Chinese Ambassador was awakened in New Delhi, and informed in clear terms that China stood alone in opposition, and if it didn't shift its position, it would affect the overall India–China relationship.[26] The Chinese folded just before dawn on 6 September. The head of its delegation, Tang Guoqiang, refused to be present at the formal NSG meeting, sending his deputy instead. They abstained on the vote, thus allowing the consensus in the NSG on giving India a clean and unconditional waiver to move forward.

It may never be possible to know the reason for the Chinese volte-face, but pragmatism is a hallmark of Chinese negotiating strategy and tactics. Perhaps China felt that they had much bigger global stakes with the Americans; perhaps they were embarrassed at being exposed and felt it was not good for them vis-à-vis India.[27] The Chinese publicly declared that their participation had always been with a responsible and constructive attitude, a standard phrase used to justify its opposition on any issue. Chen Jingye, Director General, Department of Arms Control, Chinese Ministry of Foreign Affairs, also preserved China's future position in NSG on matters relating to India, by saying that it hoped that the NSG would equally address the aspirations of all parties (they meant Pakistan) for the peaceful use of nuclear energy while adhering to the NPT mechanism.[28] China showed that it preferred to live to fight another day.

The Chinese Foreign Minister, Yang Jiechi, was scheduled to visit India on 9 September 2008. The ensuing decision in the NSG fundamentally changed the nature of his visit to India. There was serious consideration within the Government of India on whether or not to proceed with the visit, and also on whether or not to agree to a Chinese request for a meeting with Prime Minister Dr Manmohan Singh. Better sense appeared to prevail and the visit and the meeting with the Prime Minister went ahead.[29] In line with typical Chinese diplomatic behaviour and without so much as a reference to the happenings in Vienna scarcely forty-eight hours earlier and which was still very much the subject of media attention in India, Foreign Minister Yang Jiechi talked of the requirement by both India and China for clean energy, and said that the Chinese side was willing to remain in contact with the

Indian side on cooperation in the peaceful uses of nuclear energy.[30] Four days later, the *Guangming Ribao*, a prominent Chinese daily, also publicly referred to the door being opened for Chinese companies to participate in the Indian nuclear energy market.[31] India and China resumed normal exchanges. The Indian NSA M.K. Narayanan travelled to China later in the same month. He became the first senior member of the Government of India to officially meet with the new Vice President of China, Xi Jinping (the author accompanied the NSA for this meeting). Xi Jinping told Narayanan that China took a strategic view of India and that he had great confidence in the future of the relationship.

The negotiations and diplomacy between India and China on the nuclear deal and in the NSG was conducted in the shadows and never directly. India was to get a true measure of how China operated at the multilateral level. China's objective of maintaining strategic and nuclear asymmetry with India was the foundation of its negotiating strategy. It couched the issue, the NSG waiver, in terms of principle, in order to ensure that it did not become an India–China issue. This helped both in maintaining cordial relations with India and in persuading the 'purists' within the NSG that they were fighting for the principle of non-proliferation. The way the principle was formulated also left room for China to move in either direction, since it juxtaposed the right of all countries to have access to nuclear energy along with non-proliferation concerns. It was difficult for India to take issue publicly with China on the matter. This showed the manner in which China thought ahead to the endgame in the negotiations and kept an exit route that would be available if things did not pan out as expected.

China's interactions with India throughout this period were in contrast to the position taken by them during the 1998 nuclear tests. The topic of the 123 Deal and the clean waiver that India was seeking from the NSG was never raised by the Chinese in bilateral meetings, and rarely discussed whenever India raised the issue. Instead, the Chinese appeared to operate through the Left parties and the left-leaning media in India that had an ideological problem with regard to nuclear weapons, in an effort to build domestic opposition to the Indo–US deal. This might have been the first instance for China to operate politically in Indian domestic politics. China is becoming more sophisticated in its manipulation of Indian interest groups.

China never frontally confronted the United States, which was the bigger power. It worked through the strong American non-proliferation lobby and the American think-tank community. China has, over the years, developed strong networks through its think-tanks and academics, with people in the United States who can influence US policy, including in the administration, in Congress and in the media. The Chinese think-tanks flatter them by giving the impression that by engaging with Chinese academicians, they are gaining insight into Chinese thinking. As a result, senior Chinese academics have had greater access to policy-making circles in America than those from India or any other major developing country. The lack of reciprocal access at the official level in China even for the United States makes the Chinese think-tanks a potent force multiplier in the Chinese negotiating arsenal. It speaks for China, but this is deniable if it suits the Chinese government. That way there is less pressure for China to make its official position explicit until it is fully aware of the state-of-play. It was only after the strenuous efforts by the Chinese think-tanks to influence the non-proliferation lobby, the members of Congress and the media had failed in putting a stop to the Indo–US nuclear deal, that the Chinese government stepped out from behind the curtain. These were early days for China's membership of the NSG, and the final result fell short of their expectations. For India it is a lesson on the Chinese negotiating tactic of remaining in the shadows, performing the role of puppet-master until it is absolutely required to take a stand.

China also exhibited its capacity for multi-layered diplomacy. It flattered the smaller NSG members by making them feel that the bigger powers, especially the United States, did not care for their opinions. Many of these countries were still smarting from the manner in which Americans had bullied them during the invasion of Iraq. The Chinese saw this as an opportunity to stoke their fears about the American intentions regarding the non-proliferation regime, in the hope that it might encourage American camp followers to revolt against the Indo–US nuclear deal. They also played on European fears about the repercussions of a dilution of the non-proliferation regime in terms of increasing the likelihood of a nuclear attack by irresponsible countries. It was always careful to show itself as a responsible member of the international community and to couch the argument in terms of international peace and security. This is a psychological pressure tactic that China employs; it suggests that the bigger power (in this case the Americans) is a bully and it aids and abets the smaller countries concerned to demonstrate that they are not subservient. China then uses the 'opposition' generated in this way to secure concessions from the larger party, in this case the Americans. At least some of the amendments to the original US draft that were suggested by Austria, New Zealand, Ireland and the others, may have come directly or through more subtle means from China. In other words, China was able to secure these concessions not by directly negotiating with America, but by getting others to do their work for them.

China's experience and, more importantly, understanding, of how to manoeuvre in multilateral negotiations is steadily improving. It has also been a key proponent of using the principle of 'consensus' as leverage or to block progress on multilateral issues that do not suit their interests. China has been successful in changing the definition of 'consensus' from one meaning the largest possible majority to a more authoritarian definition that means every last one in the room. This allows the Chinese to paralyse international negotiations, compels others to approach China for relief and enables the Chinese to extract concessions in return even when they are the lone ones standing out. The principle of democratic majority is thus turned on its head. Finally, the Chinese never regard anything as having an ending, but as a process. This allows them to make concessions when there is no alternative, as in Vienna on 6 September 2008, by keeping larger interests in mind, such as relations with the United States or India, and to subsequently leverage their 'cooperation' in return for benefit. They are adept at generating feelings of gratitude in the opponent and in disguising their own feelings of guilt.

VI

Masood Azhar: The Principle of Consensus

The negotiation between India and China over the listing of Maulana Masood Azhar Alvi as a terrorist under the relevant provisions of the United Nations was among the longest drawn-out talks in bilateral relations. What was presumed to be an open-and-shut case began in March 2009 and which was expected to be concluded within the year, dragged on for a full decade.

Masood Azhar was born in Bahawalpur, Pakistan, and was drawn to radical Islam early on in his life. As an active member of the terrorist group Harkat-ul-Ansar, he had been apprehended in India in the early 1990s. He spent six years in custody before the Government of India exchanged him on 31 December 1999, in return for the more than 170 passengers and crew aboard the Indian airliner IC-814 that had been hijacked to Kandahar in Afghanistan by five Pakistan-based terrorists led by Masood Azhar's brother. Masood Azhar went on to establish the Jaish-e-Mohammed (The Army of Mohammed or JeM). JeM has been responsible for several deadly terrorist attacks in India, including on the Houses of Parliament in Delhi in December 2001, and later on the Indian Air Force base at Pathankot in January 2016 and on a security convoy of the Central Reserve Police Force in Pulwama in February 2019.

The JeM had been placed on the American State Department's list of foreign Islamic Jihadi organizations in 2001, listed as a terrorist organization by the United Nations in October 2001, and was supposedly banned by the Government of Pakistan. However, it was common knowledge that Masood Azhar had continued to lead the JeM, sometimes under different names, under the protection of Pakistan. Whenever a terrorist attack had taken place for which JeM claimed responsibility, the Government of Pakistan used to take him under 'protective custody', a euphemism for his lying low until emotions had cooled on the other side of the India–Pakistan border.

After the Soviet withdrawal from Afghanistan in 1990, the West grew concerned about the possibility of Islamic radicalism. The advent of a Taliban regime in Afghanistan, that could offer a base for such elements, caused a heightening of concerns. On 15 October 1999, the United Nations Security Council (UNSC) adopted Resolution 1267 (1999), establishing a committee to impose a limited air embargo and assets freeze on the Taliban. Over time, after 9/11, the sanctions regime evolved and the measures targeted a widening group of individuals and entities. In June 2011, the Security Council decided that the list of individuals and entities associated with Al-Qaida would be handled by the 1267 Committee, also known as the Al-Qaida Sanctions Committee, and a separate committee was created to oversee sanctions against the Taliban. The 1267 Sanctions Committee comprises fifteen members of the Security Council. Its task is to designate individuals and entities who meet the listing criteria, to 'lift' the sanctions when warranted, as well as to exempt certain individuals or entities from the purview of the sanctions. Any Member State may submit to the 1267 Committee listing requests for individuals or entities. Such requests must be supported by specific findings and reasoning that the listing criteria are met. It is a well-set procedure.[1] It is, however, anything but transparent.

The heinous terrorist attack by the Lashkar-e-Tayyiba (LeT) in Mumbai on 26 November 2008, in which several foreign nationals were also murdered or injured, drew the world's attention to the long-standing demand of India for the international community to take notice of Pakistan-based groups. One interesting but little known fact is that during the Mumbai terrorist attack, Pakistani handlers had given explicit instructions to kill a Chinese citizen when the terrorists sought instructions, and yet China remained hesitant to call out the Pakistanis because of their strategic alliance.[2] By that time, a number of other prominent terrorists involved in attacks on Western interests or citizens were discovered inside Pakistan, and the Americans may have also suspected that Osama Bin Laden and other Al-Qaida operatives may have been sheltering there. In December 2008, three major LeT operatives who were involved in the Mumbai attacks—Zaki-ur-Rahman Lakhvi, Hafiz Saeed and Haji Muhammed Ashraf—were listed by the 1267 Committee. The listing did not, however, contain a reference to the attack on Mumbai. The listing of the three individuals was a consequence of the association that LeT had kept with Al-Qaida. Nonetheless, it was a positive sign that entities and individuals based in Pakistan who had trained their sights on India, were being sanctioned. It was in such circumstances that India decided to apply to the 1267 Sanctions Committee to proscribe Masood Azhar, the mastermind of the attack on Parliament.

The Permanent Representative (Ambassador) of India to the United Nations, Nirupam Sen, wrote in March 2009 to the 1267 Sanctions Committee proposing the listing of Masood Azhar, Azam Cheema (LeT) and Abdul Rehman Makki (JuD).[3] India had consulted the Americans beforehand. India reached out to the other Permanent Members, China included, in New York immediately after the proposal was made. It is usual practice for the committee to deliberate on the proposal and, after examining the supporting documentation, any member may place a 'hold' on the listing request. This is normal procedure to allow for committee members to seek additional information or to clarify doubts. Russia, Great Britain and China placed the Indian request on hold in April 2009.

The Chinese wanted more information about the nationality of the three individuals. The British wished to know whether Masood Azhar was still associated with the JeM, because this organization itself had undergone many name changes. Additional explanations were offered. Russia lifted its 'hold' in May; and Britain in June. Only China maintained its hold through the year 2009. China was probably hoping that the Indian request would simply melt away without them having to take a clear-cut position. However, when in late 2010, India reaffirmed to the 1267 Sanctions Committee of its interest in pursuing the listing of Masood Azhar, China averred that it was not in a position to accede to the request. This is called a 'block', and since the working procedures of the committee state that it operates on the basis of 'consensus', the committee informed the Government of India that it could not agree to the proposal for the listing of Masood Azhar.

This first attempt in 2009–2010 revealed the complex workings of multilateral diplomacy. Although the 1267 Committee has fifteen Member-States, in reality the five Permanent Members usually settle all matters amongst themselves, and without that, any consensus is well-nigh impossible. Most non-permanent members simply do not have the wherewithal to carry out a detailed investigation of listing requests. They allow the P-5 to drive the process. If all the P-5 are in agreement, the other ten members (who are also non-permanent members of the UNSC) concur or are induced to succumb to pressure. India's first attempt at listing Masood Azhar revealed that, logic apart, the interplay of relationships was much more important in determining the decisions of the committee. Three relationships were in play: India and China, China and Pakistan, and China and the United States of America.

India–China relations had improved in several areas since the year 2000. However, the relationship still continued to be plagued by distrust due to historical problems that had remained unresolved, and new problems such as China's behaviour in the NSG during the Indo–US nuclear deal and the question of 'stapled' visas for Indian citizens born in Arunachal Pradesh and Jammu and Kashmir. The growing proximity of Pakistan to China in the first decade of the twenty-first century was a further factor in the trust deficit between India and China. Nevertheless, China had begun a Joint Working Group on Counter-Terrorism with India. Its position in public forums on terrorism, including on the Comprehensive Convention on International Terrorism, was more aligned to that of India than of the West. Due to internal political problems in Pakistan, the Kashmir Question had also taken a back seat and China did not have to publicly take a stand on this problem. Therefore, in 2009–2010, China was able to block the listing of Masood Azhar relatively easily and without any significant fallout in bilateral ties with India.

Pakistan had been an important relationship for China since the early 1960s. Over time, this relationship had transformed itself into a strategic alliance with India as the most important target, despite protestations by China to the contrary. By the beginning of the twenty-first century, Pakistan's geo-political importance to China was growing. China saw Pakistan as more than just a counterbalance to India in South Asia; it also regarded Pakistan as an outlet and a critical base for a Chinese presence in the Indian Ocean. After 9/11, the Pakistan Army became a double insurance policy for China, against the threat of Islamic radicalism spreading from Pakistan-Afghanistan into Xinjiang, and against fears of American subversion of China's ethnic-minority regions in the West. In turn, Pakistan began to depend on China to defend it, especially after 9/11 when the world began to see it as a sponsor of terrorism. Pakistan had come to expect that China would defend its actions and protect its interests in global forums, including in the 1267 Sanctions Committee. The 'block' that China placed on the listing of Masood Azhar in 2009–2010 had strengthened this impression in Islamabad.

Besides the India and Pakistan factors, the American factor was also important for China. Both saw South Asia as a strategic territory. During the Cold War, China and America had been on the same side, especially in the Afghan campaign against the Soviet Union, but it was accepted that America was the senior partner where Pakistan was concerned. Pakistan had been an American ally since the 1950s, but by the early 2000s, it appeared to be a reluctant partner in America's War on Terror in Afghanistan. America began to relook its South Asia policy and to readjust its military and economic assistance to Pakistan. On the other hand, Pakistan had secured from China the nuclear and missile assistance to compete with India for 'strategic parity', and China saw an opportunity in the withdrawal of US assistance to Pakistan, to build its own influence. Pakistan was becoming an area of Great Power rivalry. But between 2002 and 2010, the Sino-US relationship was still stable, and it was yet to become fully apparent that the unipolar moment had passed with the global financial crisis and the two wars that America had begun in the first decade of the twenty-first century. Hence, when China 'blocked' the listing of Masood Azhar, there were no consequences on the Sino-US relationship.

Five years were to pass before the Masood Azhar issue reappeared in the United Nations. On 2 January 2016, six terrorists attacked a forward operating base of the Indian Air Force at Pathankot. Although the attackers were unable to destroy key assets, ten Indian personnel were killed. The psychological impact of the attack was magnified by the fact that the attack had happened just days after the Indian Prime Minister, Narendra Modi, had made a significant peace overture to Pakistan by meeting the Prime Minister Nawaz Sharif on his home turf in Lahore on Christmas Day 2015.

The evidence pointed clearly to the JeM, which was a UN-listed terrorist entity. In February 2016, India seized the chance to revive its request for the listing of Masood Azhar under the 1267 Sanctions Committee. Significantly, the three Western Permanent Members of the UN Security Council—America, Britain and France—co-sponsored the request. This time, only China placed a hold. It thus became a matter of direct concern between India and China. The 2016 listing request was important in giving several insights into how China negotiated one-to-one on multilateral issues, which was to prove useful in the final successful effort that India made to list Masood Azhar in 2019. India also saw the repeated Chinese attempts to shelve the listing as a manifestation that China's foreign policy in South Asia was neither balanced nor neutral.

While India's objective during the negotiations was singular, which was to list Masood Azhar in the 1267 Sanctions Committee, China had multiple objectives: (a) defend the reputation of its strategic ally Pakistan which was rapidly acquiring the sobriquet of epicentre of global terrorism; (b) disavow any link between the terrorist entities and individuals inside Pakistan from its government and official agencies; (c) maintain stability in the India–China relationship; and (d) leverage the issue for securing India's cooperation on China's own concerns about 'splittist' forces in Tibet and Xinjiang. China's position was difficult. The Indian proposal to the Sanctions Committee had the potential to de-stabilize the balance that China had carefully crafted in its own relations with both India and Pakistan. Taking sides threatened to undo the work of many years. Pakistan's dependence on China alone to help its cause became an added pressure point because China did not want to be seen as 'defending' or 'justifying' terrorism. The growing divide between China and America complicated the matter still further, because China's actions might push India closer to the Americans. Suspicions about American intentions towards China had escalated after President Xi Jinping took office, and China did not wish India to get off the fence. China's negotiating strategy was crafted around its objectives with a view to skirting all these potential pitfalls.

China resorted to delaying consideration of the Indian request in the 1267 Committee on procedural grounds. Under the rules of procedure, any committee member is entitled to keep the 'hold' in place for up to nine months. By placing a hold, China bought itself some time. In discussions with India, the Chinese claimed that the criteria for listing had to be based on solid evidence, and that the material supplied by the Indian side needed more discussion. In this manner, China was also able to stave off matters coming to a head inside the committee by claiming that they were engaging with India.

They also resorted to a further procedural loophole, which stipulates, 'Before a Member State proposes a name for inclusion on the ISIS (Daesh) or Al-Qaida Sanctions List, it is requested to the extent possible, to approach the State(s) of residence and/or nationality, location or incorporation of the individual or entity concerned to seek additional information.'[4] Using this clause, the Chinese suggested that the 'relevant parties' have further communication. In this case, 'relevant parties' did not mean India and China, but India and Pakistan. This was not merely a clever use of procedure, but a tactic to claim that the listing of Masood Azhar was not a bilateral problem between India and China. Meanwhile, in their carefully worded public pronouncements, the Chinese always showed a 'full' understanding of Indian concerns, and repeated the homily about terrorism being a threat to the entire world. China, they averred, opposed all forms of terrorism and supported international efforts to end it. China pleaded that all it was attempting to do by placing the 'hold' on India's proposal was to fulfil the letter and spirit of the UN Security Council resolutions relating to the listing of entities and individuals associated with Al-Qaida. By claiming that the 'hold' was, therefore, 'technical' in nature, they sought to remove any political imputation. To the outsider, the Chinese explanation sounded reasonable.

This Chinese narrative was also helpful to them in managing public opinion in India and keeping anti-China sentiment in check. So far as their suggestion of India talking to Pakistan went, the Chinese were very well aware that it would make no headway because Pakistan denied any knowledge of the whereabouts of Masood Azhar. China hoped to utilize the time thus gained to either create doubts in the minds of some committee members so that it was no longer alone in its opposition to the listing, or to dilute the Indian asks, or both. Informal feelers were put out in New Delhi suggesting that China might reconsider if India consented to remove all direct references to the Pakistan government's involvement in terrorism and if India undertook not to make further proposals to list Pakistani individuals and entities in the future.[5]

India recognized the play as tactics. Two important high-level visits took place from India to China in the first half of 2016, and both Indian dignitaries reportedly pressed the matter hard with the Chinese side.[6] They conveyed that it was difficult to comprehend why China had reservations over the leader of the JeM being included in the 1267 Sanctions when the JeM itself was a proscribed organization in the United Nations. They questioned China's claim that its position was 'objective' and 'just'. By doing this, India signalled that it would not downplay the matter this time round, and that it was legitimately a matter to be discussed bilaterally in spite of the Chinese claiming that it was a multilateral issue. China's offer to act as a communication channel between India and Pakistan was also seen in India as a ruse to divert attention away from China as the problem and, consequently, politely rebuffed. This new approach reflected a change in India's way of dealing with China as compared to the earlier period. However, as yet, in public, India neither singled out China nor did it engage in public polemics. The general feeling in India was that China need not be pushed into a corner.

In the second half of 2016, India began to mount pressure on the Chinese to lift the 'hold'. By then the equation between India and China had shifted as a result of the Chinese actions in spearheading the efforts to block the consensus on India's membership of the NSG at the Seoul meeting in June 2016. China's efforts became public knowledge. India decided that it was the right time to take a more assertive stand. In August 2016, when the two Foreign Ministers, Sushma Swaraj and Wang Yi, met, the Chinese as usual claimed that the listing of Masood Azhar was not a bilateral issue between India and China. It was a matter for the UN Sanctions Committee to decide upon. The Chinese side also claimed that Pakistan had reliably assured them that the JeM was defunct, and that Masood Azhar had 'retired'.[7] The Chinese expected India to believe that they were actively engaged in making a serious effort to bridge the gap between India and Pakistan. This last claim about Masood Azhar's 'retirement' was simply absurd. It showed how uncaring the Chinese could be about the sensitivities of other countries. Although the Chinese are consummate diplomats, there have been instances when over-confidence in their comprehensive national power and global influence led them to adopt positions that goad the aggrieved opposite party into action. This was the case in this instance.

The External Affairs Minister of India explicitly conveyed to her counterpart that this was not an India–Pakistan matter but one entirely between India and China, and that India regarded it as important for China to re-visit the 'hold' and to engage with India in the UN to move forward on the listing. The matter was pressed again by India at two summit interactions—the G20 Summit in Beijing and the BRICS summit in Goa—in September–October 2016. The Chinese realized that their strategy of procedural delays and vaguely worded assurances had not succeeded, and, therefore, it 'blocked' the listing for a second time on 29 December 2016. In 2017, a third attempt was made to list Masood Azhar.

This time the sponsors were the United States, Britain and France. It met the same fate. China first placed a hold and then blocked the listing in November 2017. But, at least, the two attempts in 2016 and in 2017 had demonstrated that China had been unsuccessful in convincing other members of the 1267 Sanctions Committee that this was a purely India–Pakistan problem, or in convincing India that this was not an India–China issue. And it had the added advantage of flushing China out into the open as the only hold-out.

The international climate was changing fast after Donald Trump was elected as President of the United States. His desire to make an early withdrawal of US forces from Afghanistan, coupled with a belief that Pakistan had taken the Americans for a financial ride over the years and allowed the Taliban inside Pakistan to target American forces, meant that America was now willing to press hard on Pakistan. Although the American priorities were Al-Qaida and ISIS, the Kashmir-centric terror outfits based in Pakistan also became additional pain-points that the Americans could press upon in order to secure Pakistan's cooperation in ensuring that US Special Envoy Zalmay Khalilzad was able to negotiate with the Taliban for an honourable American exit from Afghanistan.

Pakistan was, therefore, already facing the heat from America and its allies when the JeM conducted a terrorist attack against an Indian security convoy on the highway near Pulwama in Jammu and Kashmir, on 14 February 2019. Over forty Indian security personnel were murdered. It helped that in a video recording by the suicide bomber, he claimed to be a JeM member, and subsequently the JeM also claimed ownership of the attack. The Government of Pakistan's feeble denials did not find much international support. The gap between China and the rest became glaringly evident when India pressed for a Security Council statement condemning this heinous crime.

China's actions in delaying a statement until all references to Pakistan or Masood Azhar were expunged also exposed its behaviour to greater international scrutiny than it would have wished for. The Americans resubmitted an application on 27 February 2019 to list Masood Azhar in the 1267 Committee. This time the tactics that China had used earlier in their negotiations with India were no longer available to it. The Chinese had to overtly tilt to Pakistan to defend it after Pulwama and in the 1267 Committee the lone opposition by China to the listing became glaringly apparent because the Americans made sure that four other committee members—Belgium, Germany, Poland and Equatorial Guinea—were also co-sponsors. The spotlight now shone on China as a lone hold-out. This is a situation that China did not wish to see. It works hard to cultivate a certain sort of public profile, where it is seen as a responsible and constructive member of the international community.

China's earlier experiences with the listing of Masood Azhar in the 1267 Sanctions Committee had convinced China that it could indefinitely stall the Indian requests. In 2018, a well-known Chinese commentator on India–China relations had this to say about this issue: 'China can obstruct India's demands without paying nearly any price, or even needs not to give a special response.' It reflected what was, perhaps, a widely held view within the Chinese establishment that India, as a rising power, was attempting to challenge China through issues like

NSG membership or the listing of Pakistan-based terrorists. The Chinese commentator's view that India had suffered a failure on account of its miscalculations of China's strengths as a major actor in the international system, did not adequately take into account that India might have learned from those initial efforts or that the global situation had changed by 2019.[8]

The final attempt to list Masood Azhar turned into a triangular bout between India, China and America. India built international support for the listing post-Pulwama while the Americans pressed the 1267 Sanctions Committee for an early listing. The Chinese understood that the listing was now only a matter of time. Therefore, this time round, the Chinese seemed to adopt a somewhat different strategy and tactics. Their limited intention was to kick the can down the road beyond the end of May, by which time it would be clear whether Prime Minister Modi would return to power or if they would be dealing with a new government. This is a tactic that China has learned to use with increasing sophistication when dealing with democracies.

At the Russia–India–China Foreign Ministers meeting in China on 27 February 2019, the Chinese Foreign Minister Wang Yi was at pains to explain that China stood with India on the fight against terrorism and tried to claim credit for the Security Council statement on the Pulwama attack.[9] He proceeded to convey to the Indian External Affairs Minister that the Pakistan government was indicating its willingness to join in a thorough investigation of the facts. China's effort was to try and convince India that this positive affirmation by Pakistan (India had only the word of the Chinese Foreign Minister on this) would lead to an outcome in the 1267 Sanctions Committee; India merely had to be patient.

This tactical argument served the Chinese strategy of delaying any discussion on the listing in the Sanctions Committee on the grounds that India and Pakistan were still talking about the matter. However, India had learned from the earlier Chinese strategy and tactics. The External Affairs Minister Sushma Swaraj made it very clear to her Chinese counterpart that this was not a bilateral issue between India and Pakistan; on the contrary, it was a purely bilateral matter between India and China, since China was the sole member of the Sanctions Committee that was holding up the consensus. The message from India to China was that henceforth there would be no understanding shown of China's position either publicly or privately. India would be prepared to call China out in public.

China expectedly put a 'hold' for the fourth time on 13 March 2019. India expressed disappointment. It began to reach out individually to the members of the 1267 Sanctions Committee to generate pressure on China. Due to India's efforts, both France and Germany placed Masood Azhar on their proscribed lists, and both were very helpful in persuading the European Union to put Masood Azhar on the EU list of global terrorists. Meanwhile, the Americans decided to up the ante by taking the matter directly to the UN Security Council. This was unprecedented and threatened to precipitate a crisis since the topmost UN body for peace and security had never witnessed a division of vote over a terrorism-related matter. The Chinese tried to use this new development to advance their interests; they see any crisis as an opportunity and rarely give up any situation as a lost cause. Therefore, they viewed the US move to take the matter to the Security Council as a possible opportunity to buy time until the results of the Indian election were clear by the end of May 2019.

The Chinese threatened to deadlock the UN Security Council by exercising their veto. They presumed that this was not desirable from India's perspective because it might close the matter once and for all. Having failed to delay this matter on their own, they tapped a common friend to help them out of a sticky situation. They used the Russians to send this message to India.[10] Russia shared similar interests on many issues with China in the Security

Council and needed Chinese support for its own multilateral agenda. At the same time, India was a strategic partner of Russia's. Russia urged India to allow the matter to be handled procedurally in the 1267 Committee rather than inside the Security Council, which was a political body. They pleaded that bringing this matter to the Security Council would politicize the issue and impair the Council's credibility. The Russians also indicated that Pakistan was ready to present a specific roadmap with timelines for the listing of Masood Azhar. The Russians claimed that it was the Americans who were being unreasonable in the matter by refusing to even acknowledge Pakistan's sincerity in resolving the matter.

This Chinese approach through the Russians was a clever tactic. However, in the decade since 2009, the Indian side had seen through the various Chinese moves. It became apparent that a Chinese veto in the Security Council would have been disadvantageous for China since all resolutions on terrorism up to that time had been passed by consensus. China would not want to be publicly singled out as a lone holdout, viewed by the international community as exercising privilege in the Security Council on an issue such as terrorism. Therefore, India's counter-response was that this matter was not procedural but entirely political, not multilateral but bilateral, and that any further delay by the Chinese in blocking the listing of Masood Azhar might have an adverse impact on India–China relations. The Russians presumably conveyed this to the Chinese.

One of the hallmarks of Chinese negotiating tactics is to repeatedly press the same point, and in different ways. While this is irritating and even offending for the opposite number, it is really intended to allow the Chinese to make a determination of their opponent's bottom line. The objective is to wear down the opposition to get them to reveal whether their position on any matter is merely tactical (in which case there is scope for further negotiation) or the final position. In the present case, all of China's tactics—the use of committee procedures, the efforts to get India and Pakistan to bilaterally resolve the matter, the claim that this was not an India–China problem, the Russian gambit—had failed to kick the can down the road beyond 23 May 2019, as they had hoped.

Now, China presumably weighed the consequences of vetoing the US resolution in the Security Council and opening the door to being seen globally as the sole defender of a well-known terrorist residing in a state that was the epicentre of terrorism. China recognized that the game was up. India had also heard about China's alleged unhappiness over Pakistan's pressure on the issue of Masood Azhar, which had pushed the Chinese into a cul-de-sac. Even in this difficult situation, they still hoped for some gain, and made a final effort to extract the last ounce of benefit before the compromise. The Chinese committed to a concrete time frame for the listing—post 23 May 2019, that is a date immediately after the results of India's general election.

The Americans tabled a draft resolution in the Council and put China on notice that it would call for a vote on the matter in the UN Security Council if the Chinese did not indicate its positive support for the draft resolution by 23 April 2019. This was known as the 'drop-dead' date. The Americans knew they had a clear majority of support in the Council. The Chinese also knew that they might have to exercise a veto. A division of vote in the Security Council, even if the overwhelming majority of membership voted for the American draft resolution, was not a desirable situation since it would mean not only a Chinese veto but also a possible Russian abstention. The Americans are believed to have offered a compromise. If China could agree to a specific time frame for the listing of Masood Azhar, the United States would not press the matter in the Council. China continued to ask that the date for Masood Azhar's listing be set for any date after 23 May 2019. They seemed to be using the Ayatollah Khomeini gambit—the

American hostages in Iran had been released only after President Jimmy Carter relinquished office so that he might not utilize their successful release for re-election—to deny Prime Minister Modi any possible electoral benefit.

The Americans reportedly demurred and insisted that China agree to the listing on 1 May 2019. China realized that it had already paid a heavy price for defending its ally, Pakistan, and that it would get heavier still if they delayed a decision any further. China did not wish to stand alone in the Security Council; vetoing the US draft resolution was like cutting off their nose to spite their own face. Therefore, one day before the expiry of the 23 April 'drop-dead' deadline, the Chinese finally agreed to the listing of Masood Azhar as a proscribed individual on the 1267 Sanctions Committee. The date agreed upon for the listing was 1 May 2019. The Chinese still succeeded in amending the text of the decision in order that references to the Government of Pakistan were removed from the citation. There was also no reference to the Pulwama terrorist attack. The Chinese Foreign Ministry spokesperson justified the volte-face by claiming that the sponsors of the proposal had submitted 'revised materials' for the Sanctions Committee to consider and that, after taking these revised materials and the opinions of relevant parties into consideration, China had no objection to the proposal. This was a way of giving 'face' to the Chinese.

The listing of Masood Azhar was a significant achievement. In public, India welcomed the decision, calling it a 'step in the right direction to demonstrate the international community's resolve to fight against terrorism and its enablers'. There was no reference to China; it was not necessary because the world knew of China's decade-long efforts to block this listing. Towards the end of the process, China was dissatisfied by Pakistan's insistence that it block the listing because China realized that it had no further advantage to gain in prolonging the matter. However, to mollify Pakistan,

President Xi Jinping met Pakistan Prime Minister Imran Khan in China at the Second Belt and Road Summit on 29 April 2019. He reiterated support for the China–Pakistan Economic Corridor as a way of showing China's commitment to Pakistan, and appealed for de-escalation of tension between India and Pakistan to underscore China's role in South Asia security. All this made little difference in the end, as it turned out, on the results of the general election in India. The Chinese tactic of kicking the can down the road would not have mattered. On 23 May 2019, Prime Minister Modi was returned to power by the Indian people in a landslide.

VII

Lessons for India

China's negotiating strategy and tactics have evolved as it moves towards the centre of the world stage. Strategies and tactics may vary depending on the situation and the relative strength of the two parties, as seen in the preceding chapters. But it is possible to discern the common threads that run through the way the Chinese deal with the outside world. Indian interlocutors may do well to remember these in preparing for talks with China.

Pre-Negotiation

Preparation of every aspect of the negotiations, both substance and protocol, is an essential part of the way the Chinese negotiate. Prior to any negotiations, the Chinese engage in meticulous preparation. This includes detailed knowledge of the subject at hand; and the careful study of available records of previous interactions on the subject, including those in the public archives of other nations. China's network of think-tanks is pressed into service to provide background material about Indian thinking on the subject matter of the forthcoming negotiation. Diplomatic channels are used to take soundings and to gauge expectations in advance of the negotiations. The objective of Chinese probing is to identify the points of possible convergence and divergence ahead of the negotiations, or as Alfred D. Wilhelm puts it, the idea is to make heads begin to pop up and to identify the targets in order to prepare tentative solutions.[1] Personal information on the key negotiators on the opposite side, especially their connections with China, is deemed valuable. Internal consultations are then held to evolve a clear strategy and tactics. This is something that the Indian side could learn lessons from.

China will always try to set the agenda for negotiations. Few other cultures endow such significance to this stage of the negotiation, presuming that they can negotiate from ambiguity to their own advantage later in the negotiations, but in fact they will then be reminded by the Chinese of the agreed terms and brought back to the track preferred by the Chinese.[2] China tries through such means to determine the direction of talks, and to avoid discussing subjects that may paint China into a corner or compel the Chinese negotiator to disclose their position prematurely. If China does not wish to discuss a matter, the standard ploy is to claim that an issue is not 'ripe for settlement'. It is generally China that determines if this is the case with respect to any issue. A Chinese draft agenda will thus contain clues on the likely direction of talks, and also what the Chinese are hoping to achieve and to avoid. The tendency of the opposite party is to acquiesce to the Chinese agenda out of a sense of politeness or in order to keep the atmosphere of talks positive, and that is precisely what the Chinese desire. It is, therefore, important for the other party to raise its own issues of interest in the working level negotiations even if these are not on the formal agenda, as a means of conveying to China that the other party has equal interest and the right to put forward its own issues in the discussion.

Another subtle technique that the Chinese employ in agenda-setting is to suggest that unilateral gestures by the other party prior to the talks may be a good way to ensure positive results in the talks. The actual purpose is to secure unilateral concessions or, if the other side is not willing to do so, then to remove the item from the agenda, thus reducing the other party's leverage. By insisting that India must totally break with the Nationalist Chinese before China would even open diplomatic talks, or by asking that India unilaterally announce the withdrawal of its military escorts in Tibet in 1953 before the negotiations on India's privileges in Tibet, the Chinese were able to remove two important leverages that India had in the negotiations with China. Therefore, paying close attention to agenda-setting and not conceding any negotiating point in advance are important in talks with China on any issue.

China also has other means to influence the agenda for talks. It employs 'non-official' means to signal its unhappiness on a matter in order to put the other party on the back foot before the talks. This could include accusations in their official media, such as the *People's Daily* calling Nehru a Western lackey, or claiming that India was acting on the behest of the Americans and the British in splitting Tibet from China. It might also involve weaving a false narrative such as when the Chinese media suggested during the 1998 nuclear tests and again when the Indo–American nuclear deal was being discussed in the NSG, that India could not legitimately claim the status of a nuclear weapon state because it did not have the capability to produce an atomic bomb prior to 1968. Using the state-run media to run negative messaging allows their officialdom to distance itself by claiming that it is not the official Chinese position. The negotiator of the other party is affected by the propaganda and at pains to avoid further confrontation in the talks. It is, therefore, advisable for the Indian interlocutor to openly call out such media reports and ask the Chinese side to clarify its view on record at the beginning of the talks, so that there is no pressure on the negotiator. The Chinese routinely follow this practice in any negotiation with India even though they are well aware that the media is independent in India.

China will also, on occasion, select the venue for the talks. The technique is called 'control on the ground'. The foreign negotiator is placed at a disadvantage by not being on home ground, but rather amidst unfamiliar working conditions, and this affects the negotiator's comfort level.[3] Thus, in 1950, China decided that India would have to come to them if it wanted diplomatic relations, and by summoning A.K. Sen from Nanjing to meet with them in Beijing, the Chinese fully controlled the environment for the interaction. The Chinese use this tactic especially in difficult negotiations, as it limits the ability of the Indian negotiator to consult in detail with the decision makers in the home country, and is an added psychological factor in China's favour. A variation on this theme is to hold meetings in venues outside Beijing. This is an attempt by the Chinese interlocutor to build a personal rapport with the opposite number in order to make her or him more amenable to the negotiation.

The Chinese prepare the field for negotiation in advance. For this, they use both diplomatic and more unorthodox means. Diplomatic means include the creation of new problems or obstacles just prior to the start of negotiations. In the 1954 negotiations over Tibet, the Chinese claimed that the Indian Trade Offices in Gyantse and Yadong were abetting the smuggling of arms. After the nuclear tests in 1998, the Chinese alleged that India was falsely spreading the 'China Threat' theory to malign China's international image. This is a favourite tactic during boundary negotiations with India. China will allege airspace or ground violations in multiple sectors to claim that the atmosphere for talks has been vitiated. The intention is to put the opposite side on the back foot so that the Indian side spends time defending itself against such allegations during the talks and is not always able to raise contentious concerns of its own. It is important for the Indian side to have its own set of problems ready to raise with the Chinese side if they use this tactic during the negotiations.

Another Chinese tactic when setting the table for talks is to lay benchmarks for the other side to meet prior to negotiations. Thus, for instance, the Chinese kept insisting that India must talk to Pakistan on the Masood Azhar listing before raising the issue with the 1267 Committee. Or that India must explicitly reject the 'China Threat' allegation before normality may be restored in relations, as was the case in 1999 after the nuclear tests the year before. It is important to insist that there cannot be preconditions for any negotiation, and to maintain this position even if the Chinese threaten to withdraw from the talks. This is also a means of determining whether the Chinese intend to talk for form's sake alone, or desire an outcome. A more unorthodox means of preparing the field for negotiations, the use of which is growing with time, includes manipulation of the media or the political opposition in India to set out their red lines or no-go zones publicly prior to the talks. This may lead the other party to consider foreclosing certain negotiating positions because, by inference, they won't fly with the other side. Such thinking should be consciously avoided, or the Indian side might also consider making its own positions public in response, so as to signal that the Indian side is also 'locked' into its own positions.

Paying close attention to the pre-negotiation process, including the process of preparation, agenda-setting, venue and perception management can be crucial for success in any negotiation with China. The internal preparation should presume that China's intention will be to place the Indian interlocutor in the position of a supplicant or on the back foot before the talks begin. This pitfall may be avoided by equal preparation on the Indian side. The Indian interlocutor must have full knowledge of facts, know his own bottom line, avoid time deadlines and, as Richard H.

Solomon puts it, demonstrate competence and control over the negotiating process.

The Chinese Negotiator

Chinese negotiators follow a pattern that was set by Premier Zhou Enlai who was both Premier and Foreign Minister for many years. Changes have occurred in both style and substance since, but a thread of continuity continues to run through the process. The simple thumb rule in any negotiation is that only the Chinese head of delegation shall speak unless she or he asks another delegation member to elaborate on a point or present an idea. The rest of the delegation is there to provide inputs and to take notes. The process of negotiation is theatrical; the head of delegation will talk in lofty terms and imbue each word and gesture with meaning and purpose like an actor or player in a drama. The Chinese negotiator will also insert a Chinese proverb or two; they know that foreigners are impressed by Chinese proverbs such as 'When we drink the water we should not forget who dug the well', or, as in the case of India–China relations, the proverb 'The one who tied the bell on the tiger's neck should untie it'. It is nonetheless important to pay attention to the choice of words by the Chinese side because these are part of an internal code that allows the entire network of institutions within China to comprehend the Chinese negotiating brief and basic position. The Chinese have been known to signal a shift in their position by using a different phrase or word to describe the same issue. This is their way of avoiding an open admission of compromise or surrender in a negotiation. It is good practice to, therefore, listen attentively and do a careful comparison of the words or phrases used in a negotiation with what has been used previously, to determine whether there is a change in the negotiating position.

In recent years, it seems that the dignified and gracious Chinese negotiator of yore may have been replaced by the assertive 'Wolf Warriors'. Of late, they tend to display aggression, arrogance, irritation and other disagreeable traits, but this is also theatre. The Chinese negotiators will utilize whatever posture they think is likely to advance their goal in a negotiation—victimhood, bonhomie and threat. This posture is usually scripted in advance of a negotiation. Words and gestures convey messages, not emotion. The Chinese negotiator is not interested in making friends for the sake of friendship. They build relationships with an eye on manipulation. The display of anger is also a put-on. The Chinese negotiator's objective is to gain psychological advantage over the opposite party before the beginning of any negotiation.

As the Chinese diplomats have become more proficient in the English language and in their sense of dress and deportment, the international community tends to regard them as 'one of us'. Chinese diplomats are not one of us. At the higher echelons, they are all members of the Communist Party of China, and owe their loyalty to the Party above the State. Diplomats in democracies act as agents of the government; Chinese diplomats act as agents of the Party. This is an important distinction. Chinese diplomats are ideological. Logic or reason is, therefore, not likely to convince the Chinese negotiator. Although many Chinese negotiators speak foreign languages with a fair degree of fluency, they almost always use an interpreter. This is both a statement of their Chinese identity and a ploy that the negotiator utilizes to think through and formulate her or his response. Foreign negotiators often make the mistake of believing that the Chinese negotiators cannot speak their languages, and tend to discuss the subject of Chinese interest in the open without realizing that somebody in the Chinese delegation who has fluency over the foreign language, is taking mental notes. In a similar manner, the Chinese negotiator may also play the boor in public. This is only because it suits them to allow the other side to believe that they hold the advantage. Behind closed doors, they are effective communicators and tireless negotiators, equally skilled in closing a deal as in putting the onus of responsibility for failure on the other party.

Chinese negotiators usually do not immediately close a deal on the negotiating table on the basis of an oral consensus between the two parties. They will refer the draft text up the chain of decision makers for endorsement, and may open up the draft text again. This may appear to be a delaying tactic, but it is usually the case that the negotiator is not as empowered as his or her Indian counterpart, and may need the higher authority to authorize the deal. It is, therefore, prudent to hold back a little before striking the final deal, since the Chinese negotiator will usually revert on a provisional deal with the expectation of squeezing out a final concession. In short, the oral concurrence of the negotiator to any agreement is not the final word; it is only the written word that counts.

As a thumb rule, the Chinese never expose their leadership to the process of negotiation. It is out of character for a Chinese leader to take any new initiative up during his meeting with the Indian side. Chinese leaders will, therefore, almost never actually dirty their hands with the nitty-gritty of negotiating, in stark contrast to democratic leaders. China's preferred tactic is to discuss any potentially contentious subject at the 'working' level, in order to let the unpleasantness play itself out and to reach a 'consensus' if possible. If that is not possible, the Chinese side at least gets first-hand knowledge of the Indian interlocutor's thought process, and is able to prepare their leadership with the right response in case it is taken to the higher level. This is rather different from the Indian leadership, which has always reserved the right to raise an issue directly at the higher level. This is a cultural issue and the Indian side might wish to recognize that it may not lead to desired results. While the prerogative to raise any issue at the highest levels is a legitimate tactic of diplomacy, it can only be used in exceptional cases in China, and only to make a point or to directly sensitize the Chinese leaders, and without any expectation of a desirable outcome.

The Process of Negotiation

It is a Chinese tradition from imperial times to establish a hierarchy in the negotiations, in order to show up the opposite party as the lesser party and to talk down to it. Former National Security Advisor Shivshankar Menon says that, so far as China is concerned, negotiations are not between equals. Instead, they reflect the balance of power and advantage between adversarial parties.[4] The Chinese use 'legalized hegemony' as a means of establishing the hierarchy with India. Legalized hegemony is the concept of a state enjoying superior status by virtue of being recognized as special in international law, which is then used as a political fact in negotiations to make clear that the opposite side is a minor or subordinate power.[5] Thus, China will always refer to itself as a Great Power, because it is a Permanent Member of the UN Security Council enjoying a higher status than India. China uses the idea of its own superiority in the international pecking order to place India in a lower position or as a regional power.

It is, therefore, important for the opposite side to be aware of China's efforts in this direction and to establish a proper hierarchy from the very outset of the negotiation. The trick is to make it clear to the Chinese side at the outset that the negotiations are between two equal parties. It is helpful to quote the Five Principles of Peaceful Co-existence back to the Chinese from time to time to make this point. The Chinese will find it hard to refute that. Establishing parity in talks with China is, therefore, critical.

One of the favourite moves in the Chinese playbook is to play upon the emotions of the Indian interlocutor. The Chinese head of delegation will indulge in flattery by telling her or him that they are an 'old friend' (*lao pengyou* in Chinese) of China. This is intended to make the opposite negotiator not only feel special but also obligated to be sympathetic to the Chinese. It almost always succeeds. The trick works best on Chinese home ground. The Indian interlocutor is told that the venue for the talks or the banquet has been specially selected for her or him, or that the Chinese leadership knows how influential the individual is in her or his government, or that the interlocutor speaks the Chinese language just like a Chinese. In rare cases, they 'break' protocol by granting a higher level of meeting than is usually warranted, to make the Indian interlocutor feel as if she or he is highly valued by the Chinese side.

The Indian negotiator is also flattered if the Chinese bestow a Chinese name upon her or him, usually consisting of Chinese characters with exotic meanings that are usually not used by the Chinese themselves. The Chinese hospitality can be beguiling and, often, intoxicating as well, and the idea is to soften up the Indian negotiator. Richard Solomon, who wrote an analysis of Chinese negotiating behaviour on the basis of the experience of US negotiators in the 1970s, said that the purpose of friendship that the Chinese offer to a foreign interlocutor is to manipulate feelings of goodwill, obligation or dependence to achieve their negotiating objectives.[6]

At the commencement of the negotiations, the Chinese always invite the other side to talk first. This, again, appears to demonstrate their graciousness and civility, but it is in fact intended to get the other party to lay out all its cards on the table first. Once the Indian side has laid out its positions, the Chinese side asks questions or seeks clarifications, all with a view to having a clear idea of India's negotiating position before they reveal their cards. It might be worthwhile for the Indian side to consider following a similar practice whenever the negotiations are held in India.

On any contentious issue, the Chinese side routinely follows the practice of enunciating 'principles' before tackling an issue in detail. This lies at the very heart of the Chinese negotiating strategy. If the Chinese suggest that both sides should first work out agreed principles, it should be seen for what it is, as the Chinese 'setting out the chessboard'. Since principles are esoteric and general in nature, the Indian interlocutor is usually impatient to move towards a resolution of the matter, and tends to agree to the Chinese proposals. This is a mistake. China uses 'principles' to create the framework for settling an issue in such a way as to build in China's core positions and to constrain the Indian side's negotiating flexibility when the specifics are discussed. In this process, China also always leaves a way out for itself, so that if they need to change their position, it can be explained in terms of the principle, and to avoid the embarrassment of making a U-turn. The Indian side might, therefore, wish to closely examine the 'principles' proposed by China, and negotiate them in a manner that limits Chinese flexibility or does not allow the Chinese side to constrain India's position on the specifics of any issue.

If the Chinese are not able to secure their 'principles' early on, they use several tactics to goad the Indian side. One tactic is to allege that the Indian interlocutor is not being faithful to the 'consensus' agreed at the leadership level. The Chinese play on the sense of guilt to dampen the resolve of the Indian negotiator to negotiate the principles. Another tactic is to question the interlocutor's sincerity. The Chinese side will claim that the Indian interlocutor is not being constructive and may be the cause for the breakdown of talks.

This is an intimidatory tactic that puts the fear of failure into the Indian negotiator's mind and keeps her or him under psychological stress. Yet another tactic is to demand explanations for things the Indian side may have said or done. This is a form of harassment or 'shaming' that is aimed at embarrassing the Indian head of delegation in front of his or her delegation. The Chinese also use threat as a form of psychological pressure. Their usual tactic is to refer to unspecified consequences if India does not relent to the Chinese side, with the further caveat that the Indian side shall be responsible for the Chinese retaliation that follows.

Once the principles have been secured, the Chinese will enter into discussion on the specifics. It is common for them to use incremental nibbling techniques (also known as salami-slicing). This enables the Chinese to secure concessions from the opposite number at each step, usually leading up to substantive results when the final agreement is concluded, but without taking excessive risks at any point.[7] Paying close attention to the setting of the agenda could help avoid this situation. Discussion on the specifics, in a step-by-step way, is usually a painful process. The Chinese side tends to repeat its positions ad nauseam on each point. This has two benefits. It establishes a 'record' for the future, and it wears down the Indian interlocutor in order that she or he may bring up alternatives simply to break a 'deadlock' which the Chinese have deliberately created. Thus, it also serves the purpose of determining the opposite side's limits of flexibility or bottom line on an issue. While the repetition of positions by the Chinese interlocutor has to be accepted by the Indian side, when the Indian side resorts to this kind of tactic, the Chinese side will allege that the Indian negotiator is faithless, dogmatic or unreasonable.

A favourite allegation that is levelled by the Chinese side is that the Indian side is not 'meeting us halfway'. It is advisable for Indian interlocutors to follow the Chinese tactic of repeating the Indian position, both for the record and to test the Chinese negotiator's resolve and intentions. One tactic used by the Chinese side is to reverse a complaint. Thus, when the Indian interlocutor complains about Chinese action on the Line of Actual Control or certain Chinese actions in multilateral situations that are viewed negatively by India, the Chinese will make the same complaint against India. The purpose is to blur the distinctions and to thus neutralize Indian 'asks' without addressing the specific concern at all.

On issues that are particularly contentious or important, it is vital to be mindful of two sorts of Chinese plays. They will keep saying 'no' for as long as possible and, by doing so, keep all options on the table. These include options that do not exist, such as refusing to recognize Sikkim as a part of India when the rest of the world had already done so and China had no means of changing the ground realities. The purpose of saying 'no' to all the proposals made by the other side is to frustrate the Indian interlocutor to the point that she or he agrees to move on a step-by-step basis. This gives the Chinese greater opportunities to extract concessions at each step. An American negotiator who spent many days with the Chinese in trade negotiations had this to say: 'In the end what mattered more than logic, facts or force of argument was that, as the negotiations had begun, the US delegation placed the "loaded gun" of trade retaliation on the table and pointed to it occasionally . . .'[8] The option of ending a negotiation without a result should, therefore, always be available to the Indian negotiator. The threat of walking out of the talks should be used only when the state of play is overwhelmingly to India's advantage.

The other Chinese play is to fall back on the power of silence. This is a particularly dangerous weapon in the Chinese negotiating arsenal to which the Indian side has succumbed many times. If there is no response from the Chinese side to an Indian proposal or contention, it would be fatal to presume China's acquiescence or acceptance of the idea. China uses the power of silence in two instances—if it wants to keep its real intentions hidden or if it wants to avoid taking a position. This is grand deception. At any subsequent time, the Chinese can reverse course, and they have done so on many issues of importance to India, including the boundary question and India's sovereignty over Jammu and

Kashmir. It is critical that the Indian interlocutor not only should not presume that China's silence is tantamount to acceptance of the proposal, but it should also sound the alarm because China might be playing the deception game. Therefore, the Indian interlocutor must also reiterate the Indian proposal more than once for the record in order to make it clear to the Chinese side that it has not fallen for the Chinese trick of silence.

Incidentally, by contrast, any Chinese statement or proposal that has not explicitly been refuted by the other side will be considered by the Chinese side as having been accepted or acknowledged by the Indian side. Therefore, not explicitly refuting such ideas out of a sense of politeness will be misplaced. Stating things on the record are of utmost importance in negotiating with China. This must be done at all times.

China is a master at manipulating time. If the interlocutor is reluctant to bend to the Chinese demands, they will start by referring to the long history of China and their capacity to display patience. This is intended to signal to the opposite interlocutor that China is not under any pressure of time, and allows them to gauge if this is not the case with the Indian side.

If there is any hint that the Indian interlocutor is under pressure of time, the Chinese will try to trap the negotiator against the deadline in order to force a decision that is favourable to China. China uses a variety of tactics in such cases. It may slow down the negotiations, or even allow them to break down. It may humiliate the opposite interlocutor by suggesting that she or he does not have the authority to negotiate or it may level the charge of 'backtracking'. These tactics can play with the interlocutor's mental state at a particularly stressful time in the negotiating process. It is, therefore, vital that the Indian side does not allow itself to be constrained by the factor of time in any major negotiation with China.

On some occasions, if the subject is of importance to the Chinese side or if they think that a resolution of the issue is in line with their interests, and if the formal talks are not making the desired headway, the Chinese will seek an informal discussion. Usually with other countries, such informal meetings are one-to-one and off the record, but with the Chinese it is more likely that the interlocutor will bring an associate as well as the ubiquitous interpreter. It is advisable for the Indian side to similarly have a note-taker and an interpreter. Somebody who had long experience in dealing with the Chinese once wrote: 'Statements, offers, remarks and suggestions made during the discussion are kept on written records by the Chinese side. Eventually everything that has been said will be weighed and nothing will be forgotten.'[9]

The Chinese have been known to make references in official talks to ideas that the opposite number may have brought up in informal discussions or even casual conversation, as if these were formal proposals. Therefore, it is preferable to clear the exploratory proposals or ideas with the authorities back home unless there is no time for that, so that the Indian interlocutor is not subsequently embarrassed when the Chinese side raises a proposal made by her or him in official talks and claims that they were given to understand that this was a serious offer. Informal discussions can also be tricky. The Chinese interlocutor will always claim that the ideas being mooted are their 'personal' view. This is almost never the case. They also tend to play with the emotions of the opposite side's interlocutor in smaller, informal gatherings, by suggesting that she or he can frankly speak about the issue. The purpose is to get the Indian interlocutor to be more loquacious in the privacy of an informal setting, so that the Chinese counterpart is able to gauge the Indian interlocutor's negotiating brief or to press upon her or him to settle on Chinese terms in the interest of early resolution.

It is, therefore, advisable to convey in explicit terms, both at the start of any informal meeting and when it is concluding, that any ideas or proposals that the Indian interlocutor has made, is her or his personal view and cannot be talked about in the official discussions. The Chinese may still make a reference to it, but in that case the Indian interlocutor can state that besides the Chinese interlocutor, his associate and the interpreter were also in the room when the Indian interlocutor made it clear that her or his ideas were personal and of a tentative nature.

One of the moves in the Chinese playbook is to play the victim. They are good at this. The narrative starts with the 'century of humiliation' during which China was ravaged by rapacious outside powers for no fault of China's. This assertion is intended to engender a vague feeling of sympathy. Then the Chinese negotiator might go on to recount how the Americans and the Soviets took their turns at bullying the Chinese during the Cold War. This diatribe usually concludes with the Chinese interlocutor suggesting that China's legitimate desire to 'rise' in the world is now being 'contained' by the Americans, and to hint at unnamed countries which are joining the Americans in this exercise. The allusion is to India. Although India suffered a much worse fate under the imperial rule of outside powers than China, the Chinese will still use the victimhood complex with India. They will also claim that India has taken over the mantle of imperialism and hegemonism from Great Britain in South Asia. Such a narrative allows the Chinese to claim that India is victimizing China after 1947. In the face of Chinese assertions that 'you are the guilty party', Indian interlocutors, out of politeness, rarely push back. This might put the Indian side on the defensive. An occasional show of aggression, which the Chinese do not expect from Indians, helps to counter this tactic.

If and when the Chinese feel that they have hit the bottom line, and if they think the agreement meets with their own requirements, they are likely to seal the bargain. There is more than one way to do so. They may let a negotiation appear to deadlock to test the interlocutor's patience and firmness, and then have a senior leader intervene at the last moment to 'cut the knot' of disagreement.[10] A classic instance of this was during the working level talks in Beijing in February 1999 to resolve the impasse in bilateral relations after India's nuclear tests. Another way to do this is to make it seem like a concession to the other side, and secure benefits in another area to offset this 'concession'. This was the Chinese hope when they tried to persuade India to agree not to list any further terrorists based in Pakistan under the 1267 Sanctions Committee provisions in return for agreeing to the listing of Masood Azhar, although they recognized that the endgame had arrived. On that occasion, India was unwavering and the Chinese pragmatically decided to cut their losses.

After an agreement has been reached in the course of the negotiations across the table, the opposite side's interlocutor may feel that a result has been achieved, and tend to let down her or his guard. The Chinese, however, believe in the power of the written word, not of the spoken word. The drafting of language to capture on paper what has been orally agreed to, and in as precise and unambiguous a way as possible, is a critical part of the negotiating process with the Chinese. The Chinese are excellent drafters of text, and they have the capacity to draft the language in a manner that introduces ambiguity or allows for different interpretations. In general, a legal representative should be part of the Indian delegation when the drafting of agreements is involved. Every word must be parsed not only for its obvious meaning but for hidden interpretation. The *neti-neti* principle should be applied in reverse to eliminate any double meanings or alternative interpretations.

It is preferable to allow neither time pressure nor the fear of failure to cloud the judgement on the words in a draft agreement. Sometimes taking a leaf out of the Chinese playbook by suggesting that it is better to postpone the agreement for another occasion, is also a way of testing how desirable it is for China to conclude the agreement and hastening the process if this is the case.

When the drafting of the text in the English language is complete, the Chinese text should be parsed since the agreement is deemed valid in both (or all three languages in case of the Hindi text). It is worth remembering that the Chinese language comes in useful to amend China's commitments when reinterpretation is convenient. In most cases the Chinese character (or word) is more restrictive than its English counterpart and thus each Chinese character has a greater specificity of meaning. Laxity in parsing the Chinese language text at the drafting stage may provide the escape clause for the Chinese side, if and when the situation warrants it. For that reason, where the drafting of agreements with China are concerned, for the opposite side it should be all about the 'letter' and not about the 'spirit' of the text.[11]

In multilateral or international negotiations, in which India and China may be on different sides, China uses a variety of tactics to keep India on the defensive. The easiest route is the one offered by legalized hegemony, for China to assume the mantle of defender of global order, and to defend its core interests by mounting a vigorous defence of the treaty-based world order even though, in many instances, the People's Republic of China became a part of legalized hegemony more by default than by design.[12] This sort of Chinese tactic was seen during the NSG meetings, or even in the discussions about the reform and expansion of the United Nations Security Council. Another favourite tactic is by hiding inside a group. This not only deflects attention and pressure away from China; it allows the Chinese side to claim that there is no consensus. In international negotiations, China is a master of double-speak. Double-speak allows the Chinese to hide within a group of 'like-minded countries', while allowing the other side to hope for a reasonable Chinese posture going forward. The thumb rule in judging the Chinese statements is that the more ambiguous or vague the public position is of China, the more likely it is that the real position is harder and less flexible.

The Chinese have a fear of being the 'only one standing'. This happens once in a while. Such a situation affects their image, which is something they have carefully nurtured over the years. The claim that there is no 'consensus' is something that the Chinese work on very hard if they want to stall anything in multilateral bodies. However, once in a while, they do find themselves alone, as they did on the listing of Masood Azhar in 2019.

In such cases, the Chinese interlocutor will make strenuous efforts to persuade the Indian side that this is not a bilateral issue, but a multilateral one. When it is a question concerning China and where they need support from India, they will never accept a similar claim by India that the issue is multilateral and not bilateral. On the contrary, the Chinese side will make it clear that it considers the Indian standpoint in the bilateral perspective, and that a stand taken by India that is contrary to China's interests will have bilateral repercussions. However, China does not extend the same principle to India when the shoe is on the other foot. Hence, it is important to firmly reject this idea and make it clear that the way China votes or speaks on issues of importance to India in multilateral platforms is always a bilateral issue.

Post-Negotiation

After any negotiation or meeting is concluded, the Chinese will come up to the Indian interlocutor to suggest that both sides 'coordinate' their public positions. The idea is to manage the narrative of the opposite side. This is to ensure that the image that China projects is not harmed in any way and there will be no surprises thrown at them by the other side in public. However, the Chinese do not necessarily stick to this principle. There are instances where the Chinese, after agreeing to a common position either orally or even sometimes in the form of a joint statement, will still add on something in their public pronouncements, or give their own interpretation to the language in the agreed text, that may cause problems for the other side. They bank on the fear of public questioning in democratic states about an agreement coming unravelled, to deter the opposite side from taking issue in public with a Chinese statement that has not followed the commonly agreed position arrived at by the negotiators. This is a risk for democratic states and has to be built into the scenario.

Although perception management is important to all governments, the Chinese have skilfully woven the concept of 'face' (*mianzi* or *lian* in Chinese) into the negotiation. 'Face' is a subtle tool to ensure that a negotiation does not result in the loss of perceived superiority or give the appearance of the other party visibly gaining advantage at the expense of China. It is axiomatic when negotiating with China to talk about giving them 'face'; however, there is never any question of the Chinese giving 'face' to anybody else. The concept has gained such currency that it is leveraged by the Chinese to extract almost any concession from the other side. The other side almost becomes a co-conspirator in the face-giving exercise, as if it is 'our little secret'.

Indian negotiators should ignore any suggestions about giving face to the Chinese by making it clear that both sides enter a negotiation to secure their interests and if that is the case, there is no need to give additional 'face' to anybody. Another perception management skill that the Chinese side exploits to great effect both before and after negotiations is by leaking stories that provide ammunition to the political opposition in the opposite party's country, which acts as an additional pressure point on the government. This was evident during the NSG's consideration of the Indo–US nuclear deal.

If a negotiation fails, perception management becomes all the more important for the Chinese. Their preference is for both sides to issue anodyne statements that suggest there is a possibility of future resolution. If a negotiation is unsuccessful, it is preferable for the Indian side to make that clear through public statements rather than paper them over, as the absence of acrimony in public is usually viewed as a Chinese gain. Acrimony in public unsettles them. In fact, China's public image is a source of its vulnerability. The Chinese want to be seen as the beautiful swan gliding on the placid surface of a lake in sylvan surroundings. Below the surface, their feet are churning away and roiling the waters for the other creatures below the surface, but this remains unseen. In this way, if the other party alleges that the Chinese are the trouble-making party, this is not apparent to anybody else and hence there are no takers for this. If, however, the fish and other aquatic inhabitants of the lake agitatedly jump out of the water in response to the furious pedalling of the swan, the very illusion that China is seeking to show to the outside world disappears, because the observer regards the swan as the cause of the trouble. One way of tackling China is to call into question its public image. It is unlikely to change the direction of its policy but concern over this possibility might unsettle them to the point where they become more reasonable in a negotiation.

The question of whether this pattern of negotiating behaviour will change as a result of the changing nature of Chinese power and the consequent perception of self-image because of the massive increase in her comprehensive national power in the three decades since 1990, is a legitimate one. The style of 'wolf-warrior' diplomacy is more strident and assertive, and optically very different from the suave and subdued way of the Zhou Enlai style that defined New China's diplomatic behaviour since 1949. The strident expressions of Chinese nationalism by Chinese diplomats on social media might bring some changes. Menon says it may still be too early to draw definitive conclusions and, his own sense is that the rise of chauvinism will be tempered by the renewed emphasis on China's past, which will ensure considerable continuity in the methods of negotiation that China is likely to practise in the years ahead.

How this will pan out should remain a matter of high priority and a subject of deep study for India.

The Chinese Players

From the founding of the People's Republic of China, Mao underscored the importance of the Party's leadership over foreign policy, and it remains the defining characteristic of Chinese diplomacy. Diplomats in China, unlike their counterparts in democracies, have to be both 'Red' and professional. Since the ascendancy of Xi Jinping after the 18th Party Congress in 2012, the Party's control over the conduct of foreign policy has strengthened greatly. A senior academic from the Chinese Foreign Affairs University has described the ideal Chinese diplomat as not only virtuous but, more importantly, as having a correct political direction and position (*zhengque de zhengzhi lichang he zhengzhi fangxiang*). The selection of high-ranking diplomats is done by the Communist Party's Organization Department in conjunction with the Ministry of Foreign Affairs. The Party Committee inside the Foreign Ministry and inside each embassy and consulate ensures that Party policy is implemented throughout China's foreign affairs system.[13] In a Work Conference on foreign affairs in 2014, President Xi Jinping laid out an overarching plan for the conduct of China's external relations, which has since evolved into the more formal doctrine known as 'Xi Jinping Thought on Chinese Diplomacy in the New Era'. His chief lieutenant for foreign affairs, Yang Jiechi, has announced that studying Xi Jinping Thought on diplomacy is an important political task for all those who engage in the conduct of foreign policy, beginning with the Ministry of Foreign Affairs.[14] It has, therefore, become the go-to guide for the Foreign Ministry in the pursuit of all diplomacy, including diplomatic negotiation.

The Chinese Foreign Ministry only represents the proverbial tip of the iceberg in negotiations. Two other players are the armed forces and the intelligence set-up. The Chinese are militarily prudent; they will not fight unless they are certain of overwhelming victory or believe they are cornered. The Chinese may use the People's Liberation Army (PLA) to posture during the negotiations, to display capability and, in rare cases, to enter into a state of 'quasi war', where the PLA is deployed but in a way that is below the conflict threshold. So long as a settlement through negotiation is desirable and possible, the PLA is regarded as a tool to achieve a political objective without a conflict.[15] The Chinese Ministry of State Security (MSS), which is responsible for external intelligence collection, is the second instrument that China, like other states, uses in the negotiation process. The MSS increasingly employs modern methods, especially digital and cyber methods, to collect information about the other party's negotiating strategy and tactics, which could be helpful to China's negotiators.

This is where the similarities with the democracies stop in terms of the players. Since the Communist Party of China is the paramount authority in China, all diplomacy is managed by the Party (*dangyuan waijiao*). The absolute convergence of the Party and State in China allows the Chinese to deploy a formidable array of other actors to influence the course of negotiations, if needed. Some of these institutions are low-key or not well-known outside of China.[16] Others are not what they seem, although at first glance similar institutions may also be found in democratic countries. Over the years, these Chinese actors have skilfully inserted themselves into the political systems of democracies and gained legitimacy, without the democratic state realizing either their objectives or their role in shaping perceptions. Since they form crucial moving parts of the Chinese negotiating machine, it is, therefore, important to elaborate on them.

The first of these is the United Front Work Department (*Zhongyang Tongyi Zhanxian Gongzuo Bu* or UFWD). It is an organ of the Chinese Communist Party that was first set up in the

1920s to unite internal political forces against the ruling Chinese Nationalist Party (Kuomintang) during the Chinese Civil War, so that the population did not focus their fears on the Communist takeover. Mao Zedong described the UFWD as one of his three 'magic' weapons. Although the principal work of the UFWD is still domestic in nature, since 1949, the UFWD has also been tasked to carry out influencer activities abroad. This is done in two ways. It mobilizes Chinese entrepreneurs, academics, cultural and religious figures to do propaganda abroad and to influence key elites or individuals in the target countries; and it persuades and even coerces overseas Chinese communities to gather information or to influence people in their countries of adoption. The UFWD has massively expanded its remit since General Secretary Xi Jinping took office in 2012. He convened a national-level conference in May 2015 that vastly strengthened the UFWD by bringing key organs like the State Ethnic Affairs Commission and the State Administration of Religious Affairs within its ambit.[17]

New regulations (*Zhongguo Gongchandang Tongyi Zhanxian Gongzuo Tiaoli*) were enacted and a Central Small Leading Group to direct UFWD activities with Xi Jinping as the head was established.[18] UFWD operates inside India in more than one way. Beyond its standard tactic of trying to influence Indian opinion-makers through Chinese business persons, academics or cultural personalities, its control over the Chinese organizations dealing with ethnic and religious affairs permits the UFWD to penetrate deep into the Tibetan refugee community as well as the Buddhist congregations in India. With respect to the Tibetan refugee community, it reminds them that they are a part of the 'Chinese family', and co-opts the pro-China Tibetan refugees while coercing the less willing to work for it.

With respect to the Buddhist congregation in India, it seeks to manipulate Buddhism through the Chinese Buddhist Association and its state-approved clergy. UFWD regards its work in India as key to gaining control over the World Buddhist Movement, which will make it easier for China to have greater penetration in other countries with significant Buddhist followers. Among the powerful tools at UFWD's disposal are the Confucius Institutes that have been subsumed under the UFWD since 2018. These are, superficially, Chinese language and culture teaching institutions, but their real purpose is to directly influence research and academic communities that publish writings on China, by offering finances and human resources to cash-strapped academic institutions in India. Even though India was, perhaps, the first country to express alarm at the functioning of the Confucius Institutes abroad, the Chinese continue to look for opportunities to penetrate the Indian higher education system. In the guise of promoting education, religion and culture, the UFWD seeks to shape Indian thinking on critical issues under negotiation between India and China through important domestic constituencies.

The International Department (ILD) of the Chinese Communist Party (*Zhongyang Duiwai Lianluo Bu*) is another ubiquitous instrument in the service of China's negotiators. It was initially established to enable the Chinese Communist Party to maintain contact with 'fraternal' socialist parties. It has since evolved into the primary party organ for the cultivation of all foreign political parties and politicians. According to public reports, it now has contacts with hundreds of political parties worldwide. As Chinese expert David Shambaugh says, no ruling party or government in the world mounts anywhere near as extensive an effort to maintain links with foreign political parties and personages as the ILD.[19]

The ILD, which is the acronym by which it is commonly known, has widespread contacts within the Indian political system. The ILD has three primary functions: first, to study and report on the internal political developments, which includes serving as a 'scout' by identifying key rising stars with potential for future leadership; second, to maintain links with political personalities whom the Chinese already know or who have visited China; and, third, to expose provincial level Chinese leaders to India. At times, it also acts as a separate conduit for information between China and other countries, but a closer look reveals that several foreign ministry personnel serve in the ILD and vice versa because there is no distinction between Party and State. Research by two scholars, Christine Hackenesch and Julia Bader, establishes how the party channel is more flexible, reaches a large number of foreign political elites, and allows for engagement with influential actors outside the realm of foreign affairs diplomacy like power-brokers or families of political leaders.[20]

Given the ILD's ability to organize 'access' to the higher leadership for the foreign political personality or party delegation, it is able to persuade political figures and parties from India to visit China, by arranging high-level meetings, medical consultations, admission to educational facilities and entry to high-profile events like the Olympic Games. Once the initial contact is made, the Chinese Embassy in New Delhi regularly reaches out to political figures to plug their narratives during key negotiations between India and China. The ILD has been able to function without constraints in many democracies worldwide, including in India, also because it has gained legitimacy by operating from the safety of Chinese diplomatic premises in world capitals.

An even lesser-known organization which plays an important role in shaping and influencing negotiations is the State Council Information Office (*Guowuyuan Xinwen Bangongchu* or SCIO). While its primary focus is to manage the Chinese domestic media, the SCIO also oversees the entirety of China's overseas publicity work through the External Propaganda Office (*Waixuanban*). Its objective is to tell China's preferred 'story' to the world on any particular issue. It manages the vast media apparatus that the People's Republic of China has built over the decades. At one end of the spectrum is the Xinhua (New China News Agency) which has correspondents in many world capitals and is a principal source for gathering information and even intelligence. Then there are the many Chinese newspapers and magazines, most prominently the *People's Daily*, through which messages are transmitted to the outside world on China's viewpoint in international affairs. The Chinese are well aware that the contents of the *People's Daily* are read by governments across the world as a window to the thinking in Chinese officialdom, and it is used with great effect in messaging on key foreign policy issues, including in the course of negotiations when its language can be carefully calibrated as per the escalation matrix. Then there are the English language dailies—the *China Daily* and its more incendiary cousin, the *Global Times*—which are wholly devoted to external propaganda.

The SCIO, at the other end of the spectrum, oversees the tie-ups and supplements in foreign newspapers which have become an important revenue stream for the increasingly cash-strapped print media in democracies. The messages that China wants to put out are carefully packaged to appear as news. The SCIO's ability to coordinate information strategy and tactics for influencing public opinion can be very helpful to China before a negotiation starts. The international community has permitted China's state-run media to use the instruments of a democratic state for perception creation purposes, all from within the confines of the Chinese diplomatic mission. At times, the Chinese media is also used to bring pressure by building nationalistic public opinion against a foreign country. This happened vis-à-vis America after the bombing of the Chinese Embassy in Belgrade in the end of the 1990s, with Japan on the Senkaku dispute and with the Philippines after the arbitral ruling on the South China Sea. The Chinese government deliberately used such public sentiment to increase its leverage in bargaining with the foreign country. The role of the *Global Times* to provoke and intimidate Indian citizens at crucial periods in India–China relations is another case in point, where the media was used by the Chinese Government to shape public discourse during a negotiation.

Chinese think-tanks are yet another instrument in the Chinese hands for influencing the outcome of negotiations. Major government and party organs in China have in-house academic and research bodies. Some, like the Chinese People's Association for Friendship with Foreign Countries (CPAFFC), the Chinese People's Institute for Foreign Affairs (CPIFA), the Chinese Association for International Understanding (CAIU) or the Chinese Association for International Friendly Contact (CAIFC), which belong to the UFWD, ILD or MFA, are platforms for their liaison work in foreign countries and to host foreign delegations in China.

Others like the Chinese Institute for International Studies (CIIS) which is related to the Ministry of Foreign Affairs, the Chinese Institutes for Contemporary International Relations (CICIR), which is affiliated to the Ministry of State Security, the Chinese Academy of Social Sciences (CASS), which is affiliated to the State Council, or the Chinese Institute for International Strategic Studies, which is affiliated to the PLA, are research and information providers which churn out material on issues that are the subject of bilateral and multilateral negotiation. According to one research paper, delegation visits by Chinese think-tanks to India in the aftermath of India's nuclear tests were instrumental in providing Chinese policymakers with insights into New Delhi's intentions and threat perceptions.[21]

The Chinese have imbued their think-tanks with an air of mystery. Most are staffed by retired or serving personnel of the mother institution, and they are often the only point of access for foreign embassies or governments to learn about Chinese thinking. Over time, they have come to be regarded as a go-to source to understand any matter due to the scarcity of public information on how decisions are made, and also because of a lack of direct access to the decision makers in China. It is assumed that the think-tanks and many of the more senior academics have informal access to the 'leadership'. In turn, in world capitals, the Chinese think-tank community is given a greater level of access by foreign governments than is the case with think-tank communities from elsewhere, which places them in the unique position of both influencing their foreign interlocutor and of gaining first-hand insight into the thought processes of the foreign government. These inputs can prove enormously helpful to Chinese negotiators. The free and open information system of democracies also permits Chinese think-tanks to publicly air their views, including whenever they wish to be critical of the Government of India, without offering the same privilege or access to Indian think-tanks or experts who visit China.

The last, eighth, agency is the Central Foreign Affairs Commission (*Zhongyang Waishi Gongzuo Weiyuanhui* or CFAC), nominally headed by Xi Jinping and run by Politburo Member Yang Jiechi from a Secretariat that is led by a Vice Minister level official from the Foreign Ministry. Under Xi Jinping, the CFAC has become the main coordinating body that reconciles the conflicting interests of the various stakeholders in a negotiation, in order to arrive at a consensus on the negotiating position and posture.

Hence, the Chinese foreign policy actors are like the proverbial octopus—eight tentacles controlled by a central nerve centre. The eight tentacles are the Ministry of Foreign Affairs, the People's Liberation Army (PLA), the Ministry of State Security (MSS), the United Front Work Department (UFWD), the International Department of the Communist Party (ILD), the State Council Information Office (SCIO), the Chinese think-tanks and, finally, the Central Foreign Affairs Commission (CFAC) of the Central Committee of the Communist Party; the nerve centre or controller is General Secretary Xi Jinping who has taken personal charge of many of the eight tentacles of this octopus. No General Secretary has made more speeches on foreign policy than Xi Jinping. New offices and coordinating bodies have been set up by him; 'Xi Jinping Thought on Socialist Diplomacy with Chinese Characteristics for a New Era' has been unveiled; and the Xi Jinping Thought on Diplomacy Research Centre has been set up under the aegis of the Ministry of Foreign Affairs in July 2020.[22] According to the Chinese Foreign Minister, Wang Yi, General Secretary Xi Jinping has made his assessment of the trajectory of the international situation and China's role in it, and Xi Jinping Diplomacy is thus pointing the direction and providing fundamental guidance for China's foreign policy in the new era.[23]

China would prefer the rest of the world to treat it like a normal state that operates abroad through various institutional mechanisms, but in China, all the mechanisms are parts of a single unit, tightly controlled and coordinated more than ever in the era of Xi Jinping. As China becomes more powerful, both economically and militarily, and it seeks to establish its hegemony over the Indo–Pacific, the interests of India and China will begin to rub against each other, bringing to the fore more and more issues that may need to be resolved through negotiations. It may become progressively difficult to extract concessions from China. The Chinese weigh their relative strength against the party with whom they are negotiating, and the process of negotiation from the preparation stage to the post-agreement stage will become important for Indian diplomacy. Knowing the adversary is important, and a study of earlier negotiations may provide clues and ideas on how to create a level playing field for future negotiations with China.

Acknowledgements

This book was only made possible because my great good fortune in passing the Union Public Service Commission's Civil Services Examination in 1981, permitted me the singular honour and privilege of working for the Government of India for close to forty years. It opened doors to worlds I never knew existed and allowed me to build memories that are reflected in this book.

I am indebted to Avatar Singh Bhasin for the vast trove of information that he has painstakingly collated on India–China relations in his five-volume compendium, which I consulted for the first two chapters of my book. The future scholars on Indian foreign policy will remain deeply in his debt. I am equally indebted to Ashley Tellis for his invaluable insights and suggestions on the two chapters (3 and 5) dealing with the nuclear issue, as well as more generally on the rest of the book. His personal involvement at a critical juncture in Indo–US relations offered me a first-hand window into the subject matter in both chapters from the American perspective. Ranjana Sengupta was also kind enough to give my manuscript a once-over before I submitted it to the publishers, and her insights have helped to make the book a more focused one.

I am deeply grateful to the editorial team at Penguin Random House India for working on this manuscript and, in particular, to Elizabeth Kuruvilla, who showed enthusiasm and encouragement every step of the way. Her suggestions were invaluable in this book taking its final form.

My spouse, Vandana, continues to be my support and mainstay as I transition from being a former civil servant to a writer and student of contemporary China. I think she knows how much of a contribution she has made towards assisting me in ensuring that this manuscript sees the light of day.

In this century, India's relationship with China will become its most important diplomatic relationship. I wrote this book because I felt that the generations to come might benefit by learning about China from those who have dealt with the subject. I hope that this book will encourage more Indians to take up the study of China. I dedicate this book to the officers of the Indian Foreign Service in the hope that the insights contained herein may prove helpful to them in their future dealings with the Chinese.

Notes

Preface: A Beginning

1. Ananth Krishnan, 'The Forgotten History of Indian Troops in China', *The Hindu*, 7 July 2011.

Chapter I: Recognition

1. Guido Samarani, 'Shaping the Future of Asia: Chiang Kai-shek, Nehru and China-India Relations During the Second World War Period', Centre of East and South East Asian Studies, Lund University (Working Papers in Contemporary Asian Studies; No. 11, 2005), p. 11.
2. Ramachandra Guha, 'Jawaharlal Nehru & China: A Study in Failure?', Harvard-Yenching Institute (Working Papers Series, 2011), p. 3.
3. Guido Samarani, 'Shaping the Future of Asia: Chiang Kai-shek, Nehru and China-India Relations during the Second World War period', pp. 14–15.
4. Mao Zedong, 'On Coalition Government', 24 April 1945, History and Public Policy Program Digital Archive, Translation of Selected Works of Mao Tse-Tung, Vol. 3, (Peking: Foreign Languages

Press, 1961), pp. 203–270. https://digitalarchive.wilsoncenter.org/document/121326

5. Telegram from Nanking to Foreign New Delhi, 2 December 1948, Doc. No. 0053, *India-China Relations 1947–2000, A Documentary Study*, Vol. 1, Introduced and Edited by A.S. Bhasin (New Delhi: Geetika Publishers, 2018), pp. 85–86.

6. Gao Guowei and Gao Guangjing, 'A Historical Survey of Establishment of Diplomatic Relations between India and China', Party History Research and Education, Vol. 3, 2011, Dangshi Yanjiu yu Jiaoxue 2011 nian, di 3 ji.

7. Prime Minister's Note to Foreign Secretary, 5 December 1948, Doc. No. 0055, *India-China Relations 1947–2000, A Documentary Study*, Vol. 1, pp. 87–88.

8. Letter from Prime Minister to Ambassador in the United States Vijayalakshmi Pandit, 1 July 1949, Doc. No. 0080, *India-China Relations 1947–2000, A Documentary Study*, Vol. 1, p. 117.

9. Ramachandra Guha, 'Jawaharlal Nehru and China: A Study in Failure?', p. 5.

10. Memo from Political Officer in Sikkim, Gangtok to The Secretary, Ministry of External Affairs, New Delhi, Doc. No. 0102, *India-China Relations 1947–2000, A Documentary Study*, Vol. 1, p. 151.

11. Telegram from Prime Minister to Ambassador K.M. Panikkar, New Delhi, 2 October 1949, Doc. No. 0104, *India-China Relations 1947–2000, A Documentary Study*, Vol. 1, p. 153.

12. Note by Prime Minister, 17 November 1949, Doc. No. 0115, *India-China Relations 1947–2000, A Documentary Study*, Vol. 1, pp. 182–183.

13. Panikkar Kavalam Madhava, *In Two Chinas—Memoirs of a Diplomat*, (London: George Allen & Unwin, 1955), pp. 67–68.

14. Letter from Prime Minister Nehru to Prime Minister U Nu of Burma, 7 January 1950, Doc. No. 0144, *India-China Relations 1947–2000, A Documentary Study*, Vol. 1, p. 224.

15. Letter from Prime Minister Jawaharlal Nehru to Deputy Prime Minister Vallabhbhai Patel, 6 December 1949, Doc. No. 0124, *India-China Relations 1947–2000, A Documentary Study*, Vol. 1, p. 196.

16. Letter from Prime Minister Jawaharlal Nehru to Deputy Prime Minister Vallabhbhai Patel, New Delhi, 6 December 1949, Doc. No. 0124, *India-China Relations 1947–2000, A Documentary Study*, Vol. 1, p. 196.

17. Pan Jiaguo, Associate Researcher, 'Establishment of Relations', Literature Research Office of the Chinese Communist Party Central Committee, *Contemporary China History Studies*, Vol. 1, 2008 (pp. 97–105), Dangdai Zhongguo Shi Yanjiu, 2008, Di 1 ji, 97–105 ye.

18. Panikkar Kavalam Madhava, *In Two Chinas—Memoirs of a Diplomat*, pp. 51–52.

19. Pan Jiaguo, Associate Researcher, 'Establishment of Relations', pp. 97–105.

20. 'Record of Conversation between I.V. Stalin and Chairman of the Central People's Government of the PRC Mao Zedong on 16 December 1949', History and Public Policy Program Digital Archives, https://digitalarchive.wilsoncenter.org/document/111240

21. 'Memorandum, Conversation of Mao and the USSR Ambassador N.V. Roshchin on 1 January 1950', History and Public Policy Program Digital Archives, https://digitalarchive.wilsoncenter.org/document/110404

22. Note by Secretary General of the Ministry of Foreign Affairs Girija Shankar Bajpai, 21 November 1949, Doc. No. 0108, *India-China Relations 1947–2000, A Documentary Study*, Vol. 1, p. 170.

23. 'The Problem of Recognition' Note from Ambassador K.M. Panikkar to Foreign Secretary K.P.S. Menon, 7 September 1949, Doc. No. 0094, *India-China Relations 1947–2000, A Documentary Study*, Vol. 1, pp. 134–143.

24. Note by the Prime Minister dated 17 November 1949, Prime Minister Secretariat, Doc. No. 0115, *India-China Relations 1947–2000, A Documentary Study*, Vol. 1, p. 182.

25. Telegram from Prime Minister to Vijayalakshmi Pandit, Ambassador in Washington, 19 July 1949, Doc. 0085, *India-China Relations 1947–2000, A Documentary Study*, Vol. 1, p. 123.

26. Letter from Jawaharlal Nehru to Sukarno, New Delhi, 22 December 1949, Doc. No. 0133, *India-China Relations 1947–2000 A Documentary Study*, Vol. 1, pp. 206–209.

27. Note from Prime Minister to Foreign Secretary, December 19, 1949, Doc. No. 0130, *India-China Relations 1947–2000, A Documentary Study*, Vol. 1, p. 204.

28. Telegram from Political Officer, Gangtok, to The Secretary, Ministry of External Affairs, 20 October 1949, Doc. No. 0105, *India-China Relations 1947–2000, A Documentary Study*, Vol. 1, p. 155.

29. Pan Jiaguo, Associate Researcher, Literature Research Office of the Central Committee of the Communist Party of China, *Contemporary China History Studies*, Vol. 1, 2008 (pp. 97–105), Dangdai Zhongguo Shi Yanjiu, 2008, Di 1 ji, 97–105 ye.

30. Telegram from Ministry of External Affairs to Indian Mission in China, 16 January 1950, Doc. No. 0153, *India-China Relations 1947-2000, A Documentary Study*, Vol. 1, p. 238.

31. Gao Guowei and Gao Guangjing, 'An Examination of the History of Establishment of India-China Relations', Party History Research and Education, Vol. 3, 2011, Dangshi Yanjiu yu Jiaoxue 2011 nian, di 3 ji.

32. Pan Jiaguo, Associate Researcher, Literature Research Office of the Central Committee of the Communist Party of China, *Contemporary China History Studies*, Vol. 1, 2008 (pp. 97–105).

33. Gao Guowei and Gao Guangjing, 'An Examination of the History of Establishment of India-China Relations', *Party History Research and Education*, Vol. 3, 2011, Dangshi Yanjiu yu Jiaoxue 2011 nian, di 3 ji.

34. Pan Jiaguo, Associate Researcher, Literature Research Office of the Central Committee of the Communist Party of China, *Contemporary China History Studies*, Vol. 1, 2008 (pp. 97–105), Dangdai Zhongguo Shi Yanjiu, 2008 nian, di 1 ji, 97–105 ye.

35. Liu Xuecheng, *The Sino-Indian Border Dispute and Sino-Indian Relations*, (University Press of America Inc., Lanham, New York, London, 1994), p. 6.

36. Sardar Vallabhbhai Patel's letter to Jawaharlal Nehru on 7 November 1950 warning about danger from China, Doc. No. 0264, *India-China Relations 1947-2000, A Documentary Study*, Vol. 1, p. 441.

37. Memorandum of Conversation between President Nixon and Premier Zhou Enlai, 23 February 1972, *The White House and Pakistan,*

Secret Declassified Documents, 1969–1974, Selected and Edited by F.S. Aijazuddin (Oxford University Press, 2002).

Chapter II: Tibet: The Price of Friendship

1. Yang Gongsu, Cangsang Jiushi Nian, *Yige Waijiao Teshi de Huiyi*, *My Life for Ninety Years–Memoirs of a Diplomatic Envoy*, Chapter 7 – March into Tibet, Hainan Chubanshe, Haikou, 1999 (Hainan Publishing House, Haikou, 1999).

2. 'From the Diary of N.V. Roshchin, Memorandum of Conversation with Premier Zhou Enlai on 15 November 1949', 1 December 1949, History and Public Policy Program Digital Archive, https://digitalarchive.wilsoncenter.org/document/117887.

3. Pan Jingguo, Associate Researcher, Literature Research Office of the Chinese Communist Party Central Committee, *Contemporary China History Studies*, Vol. 1, 2008 (p. 97–105), Dangdai Zhongguo Shi Yanjiu, 2008 nian, di 1 ji, 97–105 ye.

4. Pan Jingguo, Associate Researcher, Literature Research Office of the Central Committee of the Chinese Communist Party, *Contemporary China History Studies*, Vol. 1, 2008 (p. 97–105), Dangdai Zhongguo Shi Yanjiu, 2008 nian, di 1 ji, 97–105 ye.

5. 'Record of Talks between I.V. Stalin and Chairman of the Central People's Government of the People's Republic of China Mao Zedong', January 22, 1950, History and Public Policy Program Digital Archive, https://digitalarchive.wilsoncenter.org/document/111245

6. Letter from the Tibetan Foreign Office to Prime Minister Nehru, 16 October 1947, Doc. No. 0027, *India-China Relations 1947–2000, A Documentary Study*, Vol. 1, Introduced and Edited by A.S. Bhasin, (New Delhi: Geetika Publishers, 2018), p. 47.

7. Note Verbale from the Ministry of External Affairs and Commonwealth Relations to the Chinese Ambassador, 9 February 1948, Doc. No. 0043, *India-China Relations 1947–2000, A Documentary Study*, Vol. 1, p. 71.

8. Telegram from Panikkar to Prime Minister Nehru, 22 August 1950, Doc. No. 0203, *India-China Relations 1947–2000, A Documentary Study*, Vol. 1, pp. 324–326.

9. Doc. No. 0230, *India-China Relations 1947–2000, A Documentary Study*,
    Vol. 1, p. 371.

10. Doc. 105, Memorandum from Political Officer, Sikkim at Camp-
    Lhasa, to the Secretary to the Gvoernment of India, Ministry of
    External Affairs, 20 October 1949, *India-China Relations 1947-2000,
    A Documentary Study*, Vol. 1, Ed. A.S. Bhasin, Geetika Publishers, New
    Delhi

11. 'Memorandum—Political Officer, Gangtok to Secretary, Ministry
    of External Affairs', Doc. No. 0182, *India–China Relations 1947–2000,
    A Documentary Study*, Vol. 1, pp. 297–98.

12. Telegram, S.N. Haksar, Joint Secretary to Government of India to
    the Political Officer in Sikkim, Gangtok, Doc. No. 0188, *India-China
    Relations 1947–2000, A Documentary Study*, Vol. 1, p. 304.

13. Telegram from Prime Minister's Office to Ambassador Panikkar,
    25 October 1950, Doc. No. 0234, *India-China Relations 1947–2000,
    A Documentary Study*, Vol. 1, p. 388.

14. 'Cable from the Chinese Foreign Ministry, "Report on Negotiations
    regarding the Tibet Issue between India and China"', 24 November
    1950, History and Public Policy Program Digital Archive, https://
    digitalarchive.wilsoncenter.org/document/114747

15. Pannikar had reported in his telegram that Zhou Enlai had told
    him about China's wish to safeguard Indian interests in Tibet.
    However, we have only Pannikar's word for this, and Pannikar did
    not elaborate what specific Indian interests, if any, Zhou had given
    assurances about.

16. Telegram from Indian Embassy Peking to Foreign New Delhi,
    22 March 1951, Doc. No. 0300, *India-China Relations 1947–2000,
    A Documentary Study*, Vol. 1, pp. 503–504.

17. Telegram from Foreign New Delhi to Political Officer Sikkim,
    24 March 1951, Doc. No. 0301, *India-China Relations 1947–2000,
    A Documentary Study*, Vol. 1, pp. 509–510.

18. 'Memorandum of Conversation between Soviet Ambassador N.V.
    Roshchin and CC CCP Secretary Liu Shaoqi,' 6 May 1951, History
    and Public Policy Program Digital Archive, https://digitalarchive.
    wilsoncenter.org/document/118734

19. 'Doc. 212, Conversation of Prime Minister with the Tibetan Delegation, New Delhi, 6 September 1950', *India-China Relations A Documentary Study*, Vol. 1, edited by A.S. Bhasin, Geetika Publishers, New Delhi, in which Nehru is recorded as having said that 'we can give Tibet diplomatic support but we cannot give any help in the event of an invasion'.

20. Note by the Prime Minister setting the policy regarding China and Tibet, New Delhi, 18 November 1950, Doc. No. 0269, *India-China Relations 1947–2000, A Documentary Study*, Vol. 1, pp. 458–463.

21. Sino-Indian Boundary Dispute 1948–60, Srinath Raghavan, *Economic & Political Weekly*, Vol. 41, Issue No. 36, 9 September 2006.

22. Dai Chaowu, Zhang Jingwu's telegram on 21 October 1953 and Its Significance, *Journal of East China Normal University*, 2015, Vol. 47, Issue (5).

23. Panikkar's telegram to Prime Minister, 13 February 1952, Doc. No. 0396, *India-China Relations 1947–2000, A Documentary Study*, Vol. 1, pp. 648–651.

24. 'Minutes of Conversation between I.V. Stalin and Zhou Enlai', 3 September 1952, History and Public Policy Program Digital Archive, https://digitalarchive.wilsoncenter.org/document/111242

25. Telegram, 24 April 1952, Doc. No. 0415, *India-China Relations 1947–2000, A Documentary Study*, Vol. 2.

26. Telegram from Panikkar for Prime Minister, 15 June 1952, Doc. No. 0438, *India-China Relations 1947–2000, A Documentary Study*, Vol. 2, pp. 712–713.

27. Dai Chaowu, Zhang Jingwu's telegram on 21 October 1953 and Its Significance, *Journal of East China Normal University*, 2015, Vol. 47, Issue (5).

28. Extract from the Letter from G.S. Bajpai, former Secretary General of the Ministry of External Affairs and presently Governor of Bombay to Foreign Secretary N.R. Pillai, 14 July 1952, Doc. No. 0449, *India-China Relations 1947–2000, A Documentary Study*, Vol. 2, pp. 727–728.

29. Yang Gongsu, *Cangsang Jiushi Nian – Yige Waijiao Teshi de Huiyi (My Life for Ninety Years–Memoirs of a Diplomatic Envoy)*.

30. 'Cable from Zhang Jingwu, "On Issues of Relations between China and India in Tibet"', 21 October 1953, History and Public Policy Program Digital Archive, https://digitalarchive.wilsoncenter.org/document/114754

31. Doc. No. 0585, *India-China Relations 1947–2000, A Documentary Study*, Vol. 2, pp. 930–931.

32. Yang Gongsu, *Cangsang Jiushi Nian – Yige Waijiao Teshi de Huiyi* (*My Life for Ninety Years–Memoirs of a Diplomatic Envoy*).

33. Dai Chaowu, Zhang Jingwu's telegram on 21 October 1953 and Its Significance, *Journal of East China Normal University*, 2015, Vol. 47, Issue (5).

34. Note by Prime Minister Nehru, 25 October 1953, Doc. No. 0590, *India-China Relations 1947–2000, A Documentary Study*, Vol. 2, pp. 942–944.

35. A Note Prepared by the Ministry of External Affairs Listing the Strategy for Discussion with China on Tibet, 3 December 1953, Doc. No. 0596, *India-China Relations 1947–2000, A Documentary Study*, Vol. 2, pp. 971–974.

36. Telegram from Indian Embassy Peking to Foreign New Delhi, 31 December 1953, Doc. No. 0602, *India-China Relations 1947–2000, A Documentary Study*, Vol. 2, p. 981.

37. 'Cable from Zhang Jingwu, "On Issues of Relations between China & India in Tibet"', 21 October 1953, History and Public Policy Program Digital Archive, https://digitalarchive.wilsoncenter.org/document/114754

38. Telegram from Raghavan to Prime Minister, 2 January 1954, Doc. No. 0603, *India-China Relations 1947–2000, A Documentary Study*, Vol. 2, p. 983.

39. Telegram from Prime Minister Nehru to Ambassador Raghavan, 16 April 1954, Doc. No. 0657, *India-China Relations 1947–2000, A Documentary Study*, Vol. 2, p. 1061.

40. Report prepared by T.N. Kaul, Joint Secretary in the Ministry of External Affairs and Member of the Delegation that negotiated the India-China Agreement on Tibet in 1954, Doc. 0678, *India-China Relations 1947–2000, A Documentary Study*, Vol. 2, pp. 1100–1108.

41. Author's recollection.

42. Note by Prime Minister Nehru on the Report of Dr Gopalachari, a Member of the Team that negotiated the Tibet Agreement in Peking, 1 July 1951, Doc. No. 0681, *India-China Relations 1947–2000, A Documentary Study*, Vol. 2, p. 1112–1115.

Chapter III: Pokhran: How to Untie a Knot from the Tiger's Neck

1. 'Talk by Mao Zedong at an Enlarged Meeting of the Chinese Communist Party Central Committee Politburo (Excerpts)', 25 April 1956, History and Public Policy Program Digital Archive, *Mao Zedong wenji (Selected Writings of Mao Zedong)* Vol. 7 (Beijing: Renmin chubanshe, 1999) Translated by Neil Silver; https://digitalarchive. wilsoncenter.org/document/114337

2. 'The Short Version of the Negotiations between the CPSU and CCP delegations', September 1960, History and Public Policy Program Digital Archive, SAPMO (former Socialist Unity Party [Sep] archive) JIV 2/202–280, Bd.3. Obtained by Tim Trampedech and translated by Christian Ostermann. https://digitalarchive. wilsoncenter.org/document/110391

3. 'Letter, Homi Bhabha to Jawaharlal Nehru', 2 August 1963, History and Public Policy Program Digital Archive, National Archives of India, Prime Minister's Office, File No. 17 (1773)76, 'Biography of Homi Bhabha', obtained by Vivek Prahladan. https://digitalarchive. wilsoncenter.org/document/165242

4. Letter from Premier Zhou Enlai, Premier of the State Council of the People's Republic of China to the Prime Minister of India, 17 October, 1964, Doc. No. 2125, *India-China Relations 1947–2000, A Documentary Study*, Vol. 5, Introduced and Edited by A.S. Bhasin (New Delhi: Geetika Publishers, 2018), p. 4494.

5. Letter dated 27 November 1964, from the Prime Minister of India to His Excellency Mr Zhou Enlai, Premier of the State Council of the People's Republic of China, Doc. No. 2129, *India-China Relations 1947–2000, A Documentary Study*, Vol. 5, pp. 4503–4506.

6. 'Conversation of Cde. Nicolae Ceausescu and Cde. Zhou Enlai at the Embassy', 20 June 1971, History and Public Policy Program Digital

Archive, CWIHP Archive, https://digitalarchive.wilsoncenter.org/document/112748

7. Interview by Prince Saiyonji to Kyodo News Agency, 11 June 1974, after his meeting with Vice Premier Deng Xiaoping, in Beijing.

8. Memorandum of Conversation between Dr Kissinger and Vice Premier Deng Xiaoping, 27 November 1974, *The White House and Pakistan, Secret Declassified Documents, 1969–74*, Selected and Edited by F.S. Aijazuddin, Oxford University Press, 2002, pp. 630-33.

9. 'Oral History Interview with Sha Zukang', 30 November 2016, History and Public Policy Program Digital Archive, Contributed to NPIHP by Michal Onderco, https://digitalarchive.wilsoncenter.org/document/177549

10. Interview by Vice Premier Deng Xiaoping to Indian Journalists, Peking, 14 February, 1979, Doc. No. 2307, *India-China Relations 1947–2000, A Documentary Study*, Vol. 5, pp. 4861–4863.

11. 'Oral History Interview with Sha Zukang', 30 November 2016, History and Public Policy Program Digital Archive, Contributed to NPIHP by Michal Onderco, https://digitalarchive.wilsoncenter.org/document/177549

12. Statement by Zhu Bangzao, Spokesman of the Chinese Foreign Ministry, Beijing, 12 May 1998.

13. Statement by the Chinese Foreign Ministry, Beijing, 14 May 1998.

14. Letter from Prime Minister Atal Bihari Vajpayee to President William Clinton of the United States of America, 12 May 1998 (text of letter was published by *New York Times* on 13 May 1998 under the title 'Nuclear Anxiety: Indian Letter to Clinton on the Nuclear Testing').

15. Dong Guozheng, 'Hegemonist Ambition is Completely Exposed', *PLA Daily*, 19 May 1998, quoted in 'China Debates the Future Security Environment', Michael Pillsbury, January 2000, National Defence University Press.

16. Yan Xuetong, 'Why has India Created the China Threat Theory?', *Guangming Daily*, 19 May 1998, quoted in 'China Debates the Future Security Environment', Michael Pillsbury, January 2000, National Defence University Press.

17. Interview with Ma Jiali, a leading Chinese expert on India in the Chinese Institutes for Contemporary International Relations (CICIR), which is affiliated to the state security apparatus, published in the *Guangming Daily*, 9 June 1998.

18. Strobe Talbott, *Engaging India: Diplomacy, Democracy and the Bomb*, Chapter 2, 'The Desert Rises', Brookings Institution Press, Washington, DC, 2004, pp. 37–8.

19. Radio address by President Clinton, 16 May 1998.

20. John Garver, 'The Restoration of Sino-Indian Comity Following India's Nuclear Tests', *The China Quarterly*, 2001.

21. Karl F. Inderfurth, Assistant Secretary for South Asian Affairs, 'Situation in India', Testimony before Senate Foreign Relations Committee, Subcommittee on Near Eastern and South Asian Affairs, 13 May 1998, US Department of State Archive.

22. 'Crisis in South Asia: India's Nuclear Tests; Pakistan's Nuclear Tests: India and Pakistan: What Next?' Hearings before the Subcommittee on Near Eastern and South Asian Affairs of the Committee on Foreign Relations of the United States Senate, One Hundred and Fifth Congress, Second Session, US Government Printing Office, 3 June 1998.

23. Michael Krepon, *Looking Back: The 1998 Indian and Pakistani Nuclear Tests*, Arms Control Association, 2008.

24. 'Oral History Interview with Sha Zukang', 30 November 2016, History and Public Policy Program Digital Archive, Contributed to NPIHP by Michal Onderco, https://digitalarchive.wilsoncenter.org/document/177549

25. Statement by Qin Huasun, China's Permanent Representative to the United Nations Organization, in the UN Security Council on 6 June 1998.

26. Strobe Talbott, *Engaging India: Diplomacy, Democracy and the Bomb*, Chapter 4, 'Jaswant's Village', Brookings Institution Press, Washington, DC, 2004, pp. 75–6.

27. 'US Embassy in New Delhi Telegram 9250 to State Department, "Ambassador's Meeting with Opposition Leader"', 12 August 1996, History and Public Policy Program Digital Archive, Mandatory

Declassification Review request, obtained and contributed by William Burr and included in NPIPH Update #10, https:// digitalarchive.wilsoncenter.org/document/116352

28. Strobe Talbott, *Engaging India: Diplomacy, Democracy and the Bomb*, Chapter 1, 'The Lost Half Century', Brookings Institution Press, Washington, DC, 2004, pp. 3–4.

29. Jaswant Singh, *A Call to Honour: In Service of Emergent India* (New Delhi: Rupa Publications India Ltd., 2006).

30. Strobe Talbott, *Engaging India: Diplomacy, Democracy and the Bomb*, Chapter 5, 'Stuck on the Tarmac', Brookings Institution Press, Washington, DC, 2004, pp. 90–91.

31. 'Crisis in South Asia: India's Nuclear Tests; Pakistan's Nuclear Tests: India and Pakistan: What Next?' Hearings before the Subcommittee on Near Eastern and South Asian Affairs of the Committee on Foreign Relations of the United States Senate.

32. Michael Krepon, *Looking Back: The 1998 Indian and Pakistani Nuclear Tests*, Arms Control Association, 2008.

33. Strobe Talbott, *Engaging India: Diplomacy, Democracy and the Bomb*, Chapter 1, 'The Lost Half Century', Brookings Institution Press, Washington, DC, 2004, p. 5.

34. Jaswant Singh, *A Call to Honour: In Service of Resurgent India*, Chapter Five, Pokhran Looks East, pp. 148–150.

35. John Garver, 'The Restoration of Sino-Indian Comity following India's Nuclear Tests', *The China Quarterly*, 2001.

36. 'Oral History Interview with Sha Zukang', 30 November 2016, History and Public Policy Program Digital Archive, https:// digitalarchive.wilsoncenter.org/document/177549

37. Strobe Talbott, Deputy Secretary of State, 'Dialogue, Democracy and Nuclear Weapons in South Asia', Address at Conference on Diplomacy and Preventive Defense, co-sponsored by Carnegie Commission on Preventing Deadly Conflict, and the Stanford-Harvard Preventive Defence Project, at Stanford University, Palo Alto, 16 January 1999, US Department of State Archives.

38. Xinhua News Agency, Beijing, 14 June 1999.

39. Author's personal recollection.

Chapter IV: Sikkim: Half a Linguistic Pirouette

1. Sir Francis Younghusband KCIE, *India and Tibet*, The Project
    Gutenberg Ebook, 2015, www.gutenberg.org
2. H.E. Richardson, Tibetan Precis, Indian Political Service, https://
    www.claudearpi.net
3. 'Premier Zhou Enlai's Letter to Prime Minister Nehru', 8 September
    1959, History and Public Policy Program Digital Archive,
    Documents on the Sino-Indian Boundary Question (Peking: Foreign
    Language Press, 1960), 1–13, https://wilsoncenter.digitalarchive.
    org/document/175958
4. 'Cable from Zhang Jingwu, "On Issues of Relations between China and
    India in Tibet"', 21 October 1953, History and Public Policy Program
    Digital Archive, PRC FMA 105-00032-23, 76–81, Translated by
    7Brands, https://digitalarchive.wilsoncenter.org/document/114754
5. 'Cable from Chinese Foreign Ministry, "Draft Proposal to Strengthen
    and Develop Friendly Relations with Asian-African Countries after
    the Asian-African Conference"', 13 July 1955, History and Public
    Policy Program Digital Archive, PRC FMA 107-00065-01, 1–7,
    Obtained by Amitav Acharya and translated by Yang Shanhou,
    https://wilsoncenter.digitalarchive.org/document/114696
6. Ranjit Singh Kalha, *India-China Boundary Issue: Quest for Settlement*,
    (New Delhi: Pentagon Press, 2014, Chapter 4, Copyright ICWA),
    p. 71.
7. White Papers.
8. 'Memorandum of Conversation between Deputy Foreign Minister
    Geng Biao and Director Zhang Wenjin with Indian Ambassador
    to China G. Parathasarathi', 19 July 1961, History and Public
    Policy Program Digital Archive, Obtained by Sulmaan Khan and
    translated by Anna Beth Keim, https://wilsoncenter.digitalarchive.
    org/document/121757
9. 'Sham Democracy, Genuine Annexation', Xinhua News Agency,
    Peking, 13 July 1974.
10. 'People's Daily Strongly Denounces India for Annexation of Sikkim',
    carried by Xinhua News Agency, Peking, 3 September 1974.

11. Memorandum of Conversation between Dr Kissinger and Vice Premier Deng Xiaoping, 27 November 1974, Peking, *The White House & Pakistan, Secret Declassified Documents*, Selected and Edited by F.S. Aijazuddin, Oxford University Press, Pakistan, 2002), pp. 630–633.

12. Statement by the Ministry of Foreign Affairs of China on Sikkim, September 11, 1974, Doc. No. 2296, *India-China Relations 1947–2000, A Documentary Record*, Vol. 5, Introduced and Edited by A.S. Bhasin (New Delhi: Geetika Publishers, 2018), pp. 4837–38.

13. Vice Premier Deng Xiaoping's Interview with Krishna Kumar, Editor of the New Delhi-based journal *Vikrant*, 21 June 1980, Doc. No. 2314, *India-China Relations 1947–2000, A Documentary Record* Vol. 5, pp. 4886–4887.

14. Author's personal recollection.

15. Author's personal recollection.

16. Author's personal recollection.

17. Author's personal recollection based on conversation with the officer who had escorted the Chinese Premier in the elevator.

18. Jaswant Singh, *A Call to Honour: In Service of Emergent India* (New Delhi: Rupa Publications, 2006), p. 183.

19. Author's personal recollection.

20. Author's personal recollection.

21. Jaswant Singh, *A Call to Honour: In Service of Emergent India*, p. 183.

22. Author's personal recollection.

23. Joint Statement of the Republic of India and the People's Republic of China, New Delhi, 11 April 2005, www.mea.gov.in

Chapter V: 123 Deal: The Big Turnabout

1.   S. Menon, *Choices: Inside the Making of Indian Foreign Policy*, Chapter 2, 'Natural Partners – The Civil Nuclear Initiative with the Untied States', Penguin Books, 2018.

2.   'Letter, Homi Bhabha to Jawaharlal Nehru', 2 August 1963, History and Public Policy Program Digital Archive, National Archives of India, Prime Minister's Office, File No. 17(1773)/76, 'Biography

of Homi Bhabha', Obtained by Vivek Prahladan. https://digitalarchive.wilsoncenter.org/document/165242

3. Joyce Battle, *India & Pakistan: On the Nuclear Threshold*, Document 8—State Department Cable: 'Possible Indian Nuclear Weapons Development', 29 March 1966, NSA Electronic Briefing Book No. 6, May 1998, National Security Archive, George Washington University.

4. Joyce Battle, *India & Pakistan: On the Nuclear Threshold*, Document 7—State Department Telegram for Governor Harriman from the Secretary, 27 February 1965, NSA Electronic Briefing Book No. 6, May 1998, National Security Archive, George Washington University, between Indira Gandhi and President Johnson in 1966; Tanvi Madan, *Fateful Triangle: How China shaped US-India Relations during the Cold War*, (India: Penguin Random House, 2020), pp. 213–214.

5. Joyce Battle, *India & Pakistan: On the Nuclear Threshold*, Document 14—Memorandum for the State Department: 'Security Assurances for India', 20 April 1967, with the attached MemCon: 'Rough Translation of Revised Russian Draft' and 'Memo for president', NSA Electronic Briefing Book No. 6, May 1998, National Security Archive, George Washington University.

6. Joyce Battle, *India & Pakistan: On the Nuclear Threshold*, Document 2,'Memorandum for the Secretary of Defence: The Indian Nuclear Problem: Proposed Course of Action', 23 October 1964, attached to a letter from Robert McNamara to Dean Rusk, 28 October 1964, NSA Electronic Briefing Book No. 6, May 1998, National Security Archive, George Washington University.

7. Xiaoping Yang, 'China's Perceptions of India as a Nuclear Weapons Power', Carnegie Endowment for International Peace, 30 June 2016.

8. Chinese MFA spokesperson at press conference in reply to question by Press Trust of India correspondent in Beijing, 6 September 2007, Beijing.

9. Author's personal recollection.

10. Author's personal recollection.

11. Cheng Ruisheng, 'Trend of India's Diplomatic Strategy', China International Studies 10, 2008, pp. 20–40.

12. Fu Xiaoqiang, 'US-India Nuclear Cooperation: Double Standards', Shijie Zhishi (World Affairs), Vol. 1, 2007, pp. 38–39.

13. Zhongguo Guofang Bao, *China National Defence News*, 28 February 2006.

14. Renmin Ribao, 'India–US Nuclear Negotiations will be Difficult', *People's Daily*, 6 June 2007.

15. Zhao Qinhai, 'US-India Military Cooperation and Its Restricting Factors', China 13 International Studies 156, 2008.

16. Cheng Ruisheng, 'Trend of Indian Diplomatic Strategy', China International Studies, Spring 2008, pp. 20–40.

17. Fu Xiaoqiang, 'US-India Nuclear Cooperation: Double Standard', Shijie Zhishi (World Affairs), Vol. 1, 2007, pp. 38–39.

18. S. Menon, *Choices: Inside the Making of Indian Foreign Policy*, Chapter 2, 'Natural Partners – The Civil Nuclear Initiative with the United States', Penguin Books, 2018.

19. Author's personal recollection.

20. Author's personal recollection.

21. Author's personal recollection.

22. Chinese statement in the NSG on 1 August 2008.

23. Renmin Ribao, *People's Daily*, 2 September 2008.

24. Xinhua News Agency, Beijing, 6 September 2008.

25. Somini Sengupta and Mark Mazzetti, 'Atomic Club Votes to End Restrictions on India', *New York Times*, 6 September 2008.

26. Author's personal recollection.

27. S. Menon, *Choices: Inside the Making of Indian Foreign Policy*, Chapter 2, 'Natural Partners – The Civil Nuclear Initiative with the United States', Penguin Books, 2018.

28. Xinhua News Agency, Beijing, 7 September 2008.

29. Author's personal recollection.

30. Author's personal recollection.

31. Zhou Rong, 'The Story Behind the Lifting of Nuclear Sanctions on India', *Guangming Ribao*, 14 September 2008.

Chapter VI: Masood Azhar: The Principle of Consensus

1. www.un.org
2. S. Menon, *Choices: Inside the Making of Indian Foreign Policy*, Chapter 2, 'Natural Partners – The Civil Nuclear Initiative with the United States', Penguin Books, 2018.
3. Author's personal recollection.
4. Guidelines of the Committee for the Conduct of its Work, Paragraph 6 (c), Security Council Committee Pursuant to Resolutions 1267 (1999), 1989 (2011) and 2253 (2015) concerning ISIL [Daesh], Al-Qaida and Associated individuals, groups, undertakings and entities, www.un.org
5. Author's personal recollection.
6. Author's personal recollection.
7. Author's personal recollection.
8. Ye Hailin, 'Modi's Issue-By-Issue Diplomacy with China', *Strategic Studies*, Vol. 38, No. 1 (Spring 2018) pp 48-65, published by Institute of Strategic Studies, Islamabad.
9. Author's personal recollection.
10. Author's personal recollection.

Chapter VII: Lessons for India

1. Alfred D. Wilhelm, *The Chinese at the Negotiating Table: Style and Characteristics*, Diane Publishing Co., 1994.
2. S. Menon, *In a Manner of Peking: How Chinese Diplomats Negotiate*, (unpublished). Courtesy of the author.
3. Guy Olivier Faure, 'Negotiation – The Chinese Concept', *Negotiation Journal*, April 1998.
4. S. Menon, *In a Manner of Peking: How Chinese Diplomats Negotiate*, (unpublished).
5. Gerry Simpson, *Great Powers and Outlaw States: Unequal Sovereigns in the International Legal Order* (Cambridge: Cambridge University Press, 2004).

6. Richard H. Solomon, 'Chinese Political Negotiating Behaviour, A Briefing Analysis', Rand Corporation, declassified in 1995.

7. Guy Olivier Faure, 'Negotiation – The Chinese Concept'.

8. Frank L. Lavin, 'Negotiating with the Chinese or How Not to Kowtow', *Foreign Affairs*, 1994.

9. Guy Olivier Faure, 'Negotiation – The Chinese Concept'.

10. Richard H. Solomon, 'Chinese Political Negotiating Behaviour, A Briefing Analysis'.

11. S. Menon, *In a Manner of Peking: How Chinese Diplomats Negotiate*, (unpublished).

12. Yongjin Zhang, 'China & Liberal Hierarchies in Global International Security: Power and Negotiation for Normative Change', *International Affairs* 92:4 2016, The Royal Institute for International Affairs.

13. Wang Chunying, 'Professionalization of Chinese Diplomats and Great Power Diplomacy with Chinese Characteristics', *Diplomatic Review (Waijiao Pinglun)*, No. 2, 2021.

14. Yang Jiechi, 'Study and Implement General Secretary Xi Jinping's Thought on Diplomacy in a Deep-going Way and Keep Writing New Chapters of Major-Country Diplomacy with Distinctive Features', Xinhua New Agency, 19 July 2017.

15. Alison A. Kaufman and Daniel M Hartnett, 'Managing Conflict: Examining Recent PLA Writings on Escalation Control', CNA China Studies, February 2016.

16. Zhao Kejin amd Gao Xin, 'Pursuing the China Dream: Institutional Changes of Chinese Diplomacy under President Xi Jinping', *China Quarterly of International Studies*, Vol. 1, No. 1, 2015, World Century Publishing Corporation and the Shanghai Institutes for International Studies, pp. 35–57.

17. Takashi Suzuki, 'China's United Front Work in the Xi Jinping Era—Institutional Developments and Activities', *Journal of Contemporary East Asia Studies*, 8:1, pp. 83–98.

18. Alexander Bowe, 'China's Overseas United Front Work, Background and Implications for the United States', US-China Economic & Security Review Commission, Staff Research Report, 24 August 2018.

19. David Shambaugh, 'China's Quiet Diplomacy: The International Department of the Chinese Communist Party', *China: An International Journal*, Vol. 5, No. 1, March 2007, published by NUS Press Pte Ltd, pp. 26–54 (article).

20. Christine Hackenesch and Julia Bader, 'The Struggle for Minds and Influence: The Chinese Communist Party's Global Outreach', *International Studies Quarterly* (2020) 1–11.

21. Bonnie S. Glaser and Phillip C. Saunders, 'Chinese Civilian Foreign Policy Research Institutes: Evolving Roles and Increasing Influence', *The China Quarterly*, Vol. 171, September 2002, pp. 597–616.

22. Tanner Greer, 'The Theory of History that Guides Xi Jinping', *Palladium Magazine*, 8 July 2020.

23. Wang Yi, Foreign Minister of China, 'Study and Implement Xi Jinping Thought on Diplomacy Conscientiously and Break New Ground in Major-Country Diplomacy with Chinese Characteristics', 20 July 2020, for the Ministry of Foreign Affairs, PRC.